Outdoor Club of Victoria
Trails Information S̶

P.O. Box 1875   Victoria, B.C.   V8V

REVISION NOTES   JUNE, 1990

We advise you to note the following changes:

p. 7   Sierra Club's "Victoria in a Knapsack" is out of print.

pp. 10, 77, 82, 90 Maps   B.C. no longer sells 1:50,000 federal topographical maps.
          Purchases may now be made from local shops, including:

Crown Publications	546 Yates St., Victoria, B.C., V8W 1K8; 386-4636, fax 386-0221
Earth Quest Books	1286 Broad St., Victoria, B.C., V8W 2A5; 361-4533
Island Blue Print Ltd.	905 Fort St., Victoria, B.C., V8V 3K3; 385-9786, fax 385-1377
Robinson's Sporting Goods	1307 Broad St., Victoria, B.C., V8W 2A8; 385-3429, fax 385-5835

All of the above accept Visa and MasterCard orders by phone or fax.

p. 13   Coles Bay Regional Park: The most recent CRD brochure shows a new trail
          from the Beach Trail to Coles Bay. Washrooms and picnic facilities are
          available at the parking lot and at the new Group Picnic Area.

p. 15   Horth Hill Regional Park and area: Park boundaries and trails are currently
          undergoing changes. Check the CRD brochure and the North Saanich trails
          maps (see Addenda, page x) to identify public access routes including the
          Willow, Clayton, Littlewood, Horth Hill and Eagle Trails. Note that the trail
          descending south from the viewpoint is closed.

p. 16   Sidney Spit Marine Provincial Park: The D.O.T. wharf buildings will soon be
          removed. For information on Sidney Island Ferries, phone 655-4465. Ferry
          capacity 1990: 40 persons.

p. 19   John Dean Provincial Park: The park has benefitted recently from a major
          addition and the construction of new trails. The park now extends westward
          to Alec Road. Travelling north from Victoria on West Saanich Road, turn

right on Alec Road. After 1.4 km watch for the Merrill Harrop Trail sign on the right. Parking for 2 or 3 cars is available a little farther along Alec Road. The <u>Merrill Harrop Trail</u> ascends the western slope of Mount Newton to intersect the old West Viewpoint Trail. The new <u>Barret Montfort Trail</u> runs from the Dunsmuir Lodge property on the north slope, crosses Dean Park Road just inside the park, and follows the eastern boundary of the park to intersect the Gail Wickens Trail to the south. Travelling up Dean Park Road from East Saanich Road, watch for steps descending on the left and the Barret Montfort sign on the right. The <u>Woodward Trail</u> follows the southwest slopes to connect the Merrill Harrop/West Viewpoint intersection with the Barret Montfort/Gail Wickens intersection. Another new trail ascends from the Dunsmuir Lodge property to Dean Park Road. Travelling up Dean Park Road, watch for the trail to the right about 1 km into the park. A map of the park was produced by The Friends of John Dean Park in 1988. Copies are available from the Friends (656-9276) and at the desk at Dunsmuir Lodge. The Lodge and its grounds are the property of the University of Victoria. Contact the Lodge (see page viii) to obtain a map of the wood chip trails and to request permission to hike through the property. The trail from the end of Cresswell Road (off Forest Park Drive, off East Saanich Road) provides a fourth entry point to John Dean Park. Horses are permitted only on designated trails. Note that the park straddles the North Saanich/Central Saanich Municipal Boundary. The "Central Saanich Park" through which the Gail Wickens Trail descends is Haldon Park. By following the Trail to the intersection of Thompson Road and Mount Newton Cross Road and then turning east along the Cross Road, it is possible to connect with the Willow Way trails of Central Saanich (see below).

p. 23   <u>Willow Way, Central Saanich</u>: It is possible to approach Centennial Park by trail from the north. From Mount Newton Cross Road near Saanichton School, head south on Malcolm Road to connect with Tomlinson Road and the Hovey Road access to Centennial Park. A map of the park trails is available at the Central Saanich Municipal Hall (see page viii). A map showing the local parks and trails is also available. The Victorienteers (see page ix) have prepared a map of Centennial Park (Scale 1:3000). Price: $2.00 to non-members for a photo-copy.

p. 24   <u>Mount Douglas Park:</u> The park is now managed by Saanich Municipality. Due to the threat of erosion of the Cordova Bay cliffs there has been a proposal to re-route Cordova Bay Road deeper into the Park. A group called the Friends of Mount Douglas Park has been formed (see page viii). The Victorienteers have prepared a Mount Douglas Park Orienteering and Recreation Map which is available at the Saanich Municipal Hall (see page ix) at the Parks and Recreation desk upstairs. If using the Orienteers' map take note that some of the areas shown are outside the Park boundaries. Please respect the rights of the neighbouring landowners.

p. 27   <u>Lochside Drive r/w, south:</u> Saanich is currently upgrading the r/w from Royal Oak Drive south. A floating bridge over Blenkinsop Lake is planned as Phase 1 of the Blenkinsop Lake Trail within the Blenkinsop Local Area Plan. The plan also includes proposed pathways along Blenkinsop Road.

p. 29   <u>Lochside Drive r/w, north:</u> A circle route is possible by following Lamont Road, Puckle Road, Island View Road and Homathko Drive. The grounds of the Saanich Historical Artifacts Society (see page ix) now include nature trails and picnic grounds. Hours are 8:30 - noon (8:30 - 4:00 summer). Donations welcome. Wheelchair accessible.

p. 29   <u>Island View Beach Regional Park:</u> The toilet building at the north end of Homathko Drive is now wheelchair accessible.

p. 30   **"Gateway to Victoria's Beaches"** by Barbara Chapman (1976) is listed in the Victoria Public Library pamphlet file under: Victoria-Beaches.

p. 32   <u>Bear Hill Park:</u> Erratum: The Odyssey Road designation belongs on the dotted trail line, not the Park boundary line. Note that the trail to Central Saanich Road is very rough, and that the Summit Trail from Bear Hill Road is steep and rocky.

p. 32   <u>Elk/Beaver Lake Regional Park:</u> On the west side of Elk Lake, Doyle Road now connects with Forest Hill Road. At the point where the old Forest Hill Road meets the new extension, a public trail leads down a rough path to the lakeside trail. Where the sharp left-hand bend on Linnet Lane occurs, there is access to Beaver Lake Park on a bridle/hiking trail connecting with the lakeside trail. Access to the park is also possible from Townsend Drive to the right (east) just before the intersection with Aurora Way. The beach access at Hamsterly Beach is specially designed for those with disabling handicaps.

p. 34   <u>Colquitz River Linear Park:</u> Note that Cuthbert Holmes Park (see page x) has been developed behind the Tillicum Mall. There are still no bridges over the ditches in the Panama Flats so it is still necessary to detour there, but it is now possible to walk along the river from Copley Park to Lindsay Street without detouring along Mann Avenue and Markham Street. There is a new, signed trail from Wilkinson Road, near the Lindsay Street intersection, down to Quick's Bottom.

p. 37   <u>Swan Lake:</u> The new Nature House has been built and is open the year round, Saturdays and Sundays 12 - 4 p.m., weekdays 8:30 a.m. - 4 p.m. The Swan Lake trails have been upgraded for year-round use. The old parking lot near the Nature House is for handicapped parking only. Nature House and toilets are wheelchair accessible. The new parking lot is at the corner of Swan Lake Road and Ralph Street. Christmas Hill is a very fragile area. The Christmas Hill trail up Nelthorpe and into the Sanctuary is still under construction and is not yet open to the public. Public access is possible off Nicholson Street (signed). No dogs are allowed in the Sanctuary.

pp. 38-41   Mount Work Regional Park: A new access road is being constructed from Wallace Drive, near Farmington Road, to Durrance Road near its intersection with Willis Point Road. If you park at the P nearest Pease Lake (p. 40) and head down the Timberman Trail toward the Bight, you may choose one of three trails: (1) the Nature Trail (Maidenhair Trail), descends alongside McKenzie Creek and joins the McKenzie Bight Trail; (2) the Cascade Trail descends along the east side of Pease Creek, crosses McKenzie Creek, and joins the McKenzie Bight Trail; (3) roughly parallels the Cascade Trail, following the west side of the creek, coming out above the beach to the south side of McKenzie Creek. If you wish to ascend from this point and are standing here with your back to the beach, you are presented with three trails. On your right is the trail to Elbow Point. On your left is the trail just described above. The trail in the middle is a very steep boring grind up an old logging road. Close to the top it disappears and leaves you to bushwhack through to the Timberman Trail. This route, as shown on the map, p. 40, is not recommended. Once back on the Timberman (main) Trail, note that the trail heads out of the park and climbs toward Jocelyn Hill and the Gowlland Range.

p. 42   Lone Tree Hill Regional Park: Off-road parking lot.

p. 43   Thomas Francis/Freeman King Regional Park: Horses and bicycles are not permitted on park trails.

p. 47   Thetis Lake Park: Spring tours of the Sanctuary are no longer offered. There is an information board near the entrance to the park that shows pictures and names of the wild flowers and a map of the trails in the park, with suggested hiking times for each trail. Please note: it is not recommended that hikers try to cross Highway 1 to gain access to Mill Hill. Currently there is a proposal to construct a major highway interchange near the entrance to the park. The Victorienteers have produced a coloured contour map (Scale 1:10,000) of the park. Price: $3.00 to non-members.

p. 51   Mill Hill Regional Park: Note caution above; attempts to cross the Trans-Canada Highway are not recommended. This section of the C.N.R. r/w has been developed as part of the Galloping Goose Corridor (see pages v and vi). Major changes to the Trans-Canada Highway interchanges are proposed.

p. 52   Goldstream Provincial Park: The Park brochures are available at the Nature House or the Gate House. The trail from the parking lot to the Nature House and the Nature House itself are wheelchair accessible. A loop trail along the river will be made wheelchair accessible during 1990 in time for the fall spawning. Please avoid the Upper Goldstream Trail in the Campground area during spawning season. The coho and chinook that spawn in the upper reaches are returning in such low numbers that human intrusion must be avoided. To avoid trespass, stay on the designated trail if climbing Mount Finlayson.

p. 57   <u>Witty's Lagoon Regional Park:</u> Washrooms, Nature House, picnic area, waterfalls overlook and trail are wheelchair accessible. Special handicapped parking is available at the Nature House via the service road. Phone the Capital Regional Parks office (see p. 90) for hours when Nature House and road are open.

p. 59   <u>Devonian Regional Park:</u> The new CRD brochure includes Witty's Lagoon and Albert Head Lagoon Regional Parks.

p. 60   <u>East Sooke Regional Park:</u> If approaching the park via Coppermine Road, the "dirt road" shown on Map 20 is Gordon Road (signed). The Victorienteers have produced an excellent map of the Aylard Farm area of the park. Price: $2.00 to non-members for a photo-copy. Aylard Farm area and toilets are the only part of the park suitable for wheelchair use.

pp. 65-79   <u>Abandoned C.N.R. r/w:</u> Note that this section of the r/w from Atkins Road to Leechtown is being developed as the <u>Galloping Goose Regional Park Corridor</u> and change all references accordingly. A CRD brochure is available. Please up-date your copy of the brochure as follows: (1) the section to the east of Sooke Road between Nob Hill Road and Aldeane Avenue (maps 16 and 22) is to be avoided due to danger in attempting to cross Sooke Road; (2) the bridges at Veitch Creek and Stony Creek will be built by the end of 1990; but, (3) the trestles over Charters River and Todd Creek have not passed inspection, so the Sooke River Railway Preservation Society no longer operates its railway service. Facilities are being upgraded along the Park Corridor.

p. 67   <u>Map 21 - Tillicum Mall to Highway Interchange:</u> Note that Cuthbert Holmes Park (see page x) has been developed behind the Tillicum Mall. Parts of this section of the r/w may be used for the proposed upgrading of the Trans-Canada Highway and major changes are proposed for Highway intersections. At present, Craigflower Creek may be crossed by taking Creed Road and a new street, Watkiss Way, with a good bridge.

p. 67   <u>May 16 - Highway Interchange to Colwood Corners:</u> Improvements to this section of the Corridor have eliminated all need for detours. The bridge over the Millstream is not suitable for horses. Note caution above (pp. 65-79) against attempting to cross Sooke Road.

---

p. 69   <u>Map 22 - Colwood Corners to Happy Valley Road:</u> Note caution above, pp. 65-79 (page v), against attempting to cross Sooke Road. Improvements include bridges over Bilston Creek near Luxton Road and Winter Road. Surfacing in rock screenings makes the Corridor wheelchair accessible from Jacklin Road to the Luxton Fairgrounds. Note that Glen Cove Park lies between Glen Lake and the Corridor.

p. 71   <u>Map 23 - Happy Valley Road to Matheson Lake Park:</u> The bridge is in over Metchosin Creek.

p. 73   <u>Matheson Lake Provincial Park:</u> Bridges over Wildwood Creek and Matheson Creek have been built.

p. 75   <u>Roche Cove Regional Park:</u> The trail from the parking lot to Cedar Grove Trail is more accurately depicted on the CRD brochure. Toilet facilities are wheelchair accessible. The Galloping Goose Trail will be passable through this entire section with the completion of the Veitch Creek and Ayum (Stony) Creek bridges in 1990 or 1991. Part of the Crown Land abutting Roche Cove Regional Park and Matheson Lake Provincial Park has been added to Roche Cove Regional Park. (Maps 24 and 25.)

pp. 76-79   <u>CNR Right-of-way,</u> etc. Facilities are being provided along the Corridor. See note above, pp. 65-79 (page v), about Sooke River Railway Preservation Society. A Victorienteers map of Camp Thunderbird is available. Price: $3.00 to non-members. Map 92B/5 is available from Maps B.C. only in a scale of 1:125,000. See note above (page i) for other map sources. Outdoor Recreation Council Map #15 is out of print. The former CIP (given as Canadian Industrial Products Inc.) is now Canadian Pacific Forest Products (see pages viii and 91). They and six other private and public organizations have cooperated to produce the **"Guide to Forest Land of Southern Vancouver Island"**, which is a map showing roads and recreational opportunities in the Lake Cowichan Combined Fire Organization (Port Alberni south). Free copies may be picked up at several outlets including the C.P.F.P. and Western Forest Products offices, and Gordon's Sporting Goods.

p. 82   <u>Spectacle/Oliphant Lakes:</u> See note above (page i) for new sources of Map 92B/12, scale 1:50,000. The Outdoor Recreation Council Map #15 is now out of print.

pp. 83-85   <u>Beach Access From Highway #14 West of Sooke</u>

<u>French Beach Provincial Park:</u> There is a new adventure playground.

<u>Jordan River (WFP Ltd.):</u> The picnic site is now a Recreation Site with park facilities including fire pits and picnic tables.

China Beach Provincial Park: Please, no fires.

Mystic Beach Trail (WFP Ltd., TFL 25): The steep trail leads to a lovely sandy beach with interesting rock formations and a waterfall.

Map 28 - Sombrio Beach Trails (WFP Ltd., TFL 25): Two trails lead down to the beach with signs showing the way from the highway. (1) is the Sombrio East Trail. Some sections can be muddy in the wet season. (2) is the Sombrio West Trail, which now comes out to the beach close to the mouth of the Sombrio River instead of near the middle of the beach as shown on the map. The **"Visitors' Guide to Jordan River Area"** is still available from Western Forest Products Ltd. The company regularly maintains all of their recreation sites and trails.

p. 87 Botanical Beach (Port Renfrew): This is now a Provincial Park with some facilities. The road from Victoria via Sooke and Jordan River is paved and usually in good condition. **"Pacific Coast Tide and Current Tables"** is available from the Canadian Hydrographic Service (9860 West Saanich Road) c/o Chart Sales & Distribution (phone: 356-6358), or by mail (see p. 87), at a price of $6.00 plus 6% B.C. Provincial Sales Tax. It is also available at the same price through marine chandlers. Specific public inquiries will be answered by the Tidal Information Branch (356-6371) but they prefer that you refer to the tables yourself. The 2-hectare area at Botanical Beach is now part of the Park. A B.C. Parks brochure is available at the Port Renfrew Info Centre. Please do not remove any living thing from the Park.

p. 89 The West Coast Trail: A Canadian Parks Information Centre at Port Renfrew (647-5434), Pachena Bay (728-3234), or Long Beach (726-4212) should be contacted for a free information package. In May, 1990, two new regulations went into effect: (1) backpackers will be required to register and obtain a free permit prior to commencing their hike on the trail; (2) maximum group size is now 10 people. The waterproof topographical map **"West Coast Trail, Port Renfrew-Bamfield"** scale 1:50,000 is one of the few maps in this scale still carried by Maps B.C. New price: $4.50 Cdn. (B.C. residents only - add 6% sales tax) plus $1 handling/shipping in B.C., $3 rest of Canada; $5 outside of Canada. It is also available at other outlets (see page i). Obee's **"The Pacific Explorer"** is available in a new edition, from Whitecap Books (see page ix). A 6th revised edition (1990) of the **"The West Coast Trail and Nitinat Lakes: A Trail Guide by the Sierra Club of British Columbia"** is available at a price of $9.95 (see page ix). A new book from Cloudcap Books (see page viii), **"Blisters and Bliss"**, by Wayne Aitken and David Foster with illustrations by Nelson Dewey, is priced locally at $11.95. The Pack and Boots Shop has closed but you can still use the notice board at the Youth Hostel with permission from the person at the front desk.

pp. 90-91   Pack and Boots Shop closed - delete store phone number. Maps B.C. (see page i) now Map & Air Photo Sales, Ministry of Crown Lands, 553 Superior Street, Victoria, B.C., V8V 1X4 (387-1441).

B.C. Parks now B.C. Ministry of Parks, 4000 Seymour Place, Victoria, B.C. V8V 1X4 (387-5002). For information on South Vancouver Island Provincial Parks, contact the Malahat District Office, 2930 Trans-Canada Highway, R.R. 6, Victoria, B.C., V8X 3X2 (387-4363).

Ministry of Forests and Lands now B.C. Ministry of Forests. Their Public Affairs Branch is at 595 Pandora Ave., Victoria, B.C., V8W 3E7 (387-5255). The CRD Parks Division has a phone number for a recorded parks information message: 474-PARK (474-7275). Brochures about CRD parks facilities and programs are available.

The former CIP (given as Canadian Industrial Products) is now Canadian Pacific Forest Products (address and phone number unchanged.)

Outdoor Recreation Council of B.C. now at 334 - 1367 West Broadway, Vancouver, B.C., V6H 4A7 (737-3058). Their Map #15, "Greater Victoria-Gulf Islands-Nanaimo Region" now out of print.

Add:

Central Saanich Municipal Hall, Recreation Dept., 1903 Mt. Newton Cross Road, Saanichton, B.C., V0S 1M0 (652-4444).

Cloudcap Books, Box 27344, Seattle, WA 98125, U.S.A.

Colwood City Hall, Planning Dept., 3300 Wishart Road, Victoria, B.C., V9C 1R1 (478-5590).

Dunsmuir Lodge, 1515 McTavish Road, Sidney, B.C., V8L 3Y3 (656-3166).

Esquimalt Parks and Recreation Commission, 1149A Esquimalt Road (in the new library building), Victoria, B.C., V9A 3N6 (386-6128).

Fort Rodd Hill National Historic Park, 603 Fort Rodd Hill Road, Victoria, B.C., V9C 2W8 (380-4662)

Friends of Mount Douglas Park, c/o 4623 Cordova Bay Road, Victoria, B.C., V8X 3V6 (658-5039 or 658-5873).

Gordon's Sporting Goods, 1030 Hillside Ave., Victoria, B.C., V8T 2A3 (382-5815).

Henderson Recreation Centre, 2291 Cedar Hill Cross Road, Victoria, B.C., V8R 5E6 (595-7946).

Juan de Fuca Recreation Centre, 1767 Island Highway, Victoria, B.C., V9B 1J1 (478-8384).

Metchosin District Municipal Hall, 4450 Happy Valley Road, R.R.1 Victoria, B.C., V8X 3W9 (474-3167).

North Saanich Municipal Hall, 1620 Mills Road, Sidney (mail: Box 2639, Sidney, B.C. V8L 4C1), (656-0781).

Royal Roads Military College, Sooke Road, Victoria (mail: FMO, Victoria, B.C., V0S 1B0), (380-4660).

Saanich Historical Artifacts Society, 7321 Lochside Drive, Saanichton (mail: Box 134, Saanichton, B.C. V0S 1M0), (652-5522).

Saanich Municipal Hall, Parks and Recreation Dept., 770 Vernon Avenue, Victoria, B.C., V8X 2W7 (386-2241).

Sierra Club of B.C., 314 - 620 View St., Victoria, B.C., V8W 1J6 (386-5255 or 386-2153); fax: 386-4453).

Sierra Ecology House (in Market Square), 106 - 560 Johnson St., Victoria, B.C., V8W 3C6, (384-1654).

Sunset Riding Club, c/o 1365 Laurel Road, R.R.3, Sidney, B.C., V8L 3X9 (656-5318).

University of Victoria, Finnerty Road, Victoria (mail: P.O. Box 1700, Victoria, B.C., V8W 2Y2), (721-7211).

City of Victoria, Dept. of Parks and Recreation, 633 Pandora Ave., Victoria, B.C. V8P 1P6 (384-7713).

Victorienteers Orienteering Club, P.O. Box 6433, Postal Depot #1, Victoria, B.C., V8P 5M3 (Carl Coger, 380-6562 or 477-8317).

View Royal Town Hall, 45 View Royal Avenue, Victoria, B.C., V9B 1A6 (479-6800).

Whitecap Books, 1086 West 3rd, North Vancouver, B.C., V7P 3J6.

ADDENDA

<u>North Saanich:</u> A 6-page set of hand-drawn maps showing parks, trails and beach access is available at the North Saanich Municipal Hall (see page ix). Areas covered so far include Deep Cove, Cloake Hill, Ardmore, Patricia Bay, Horth Hill and Curteis Point. More to follow.

<u>Saanich:</u> **"Discover Saanich Trails and Walkways"** is a 3-page inventory which classifies each trail by length in metres of hog fuel, granite screenings, or concrete/asphalt surfacing. **"Discover Saanich Parks and Recreation"** is a one-page colour map and guide to 99 parks and numerous facilities within the Municipality. If you should ever wonder if your local short-cut is actually public property, you may consult a hefty book of maps. All are available in the Parks and Recreation Department, upstairs at the Municipal Hall (see page ix). In addition to the trails already described in **"Hiking Trails I"**, we recommend <u>Mount Tolmie</u> for a good climb and a view. The <u>Gorge Waterway</u>, which is well-lit for a late evening stroll, is wheel-chair accessible and connects with Esquimalt parks via the bridge over the Gorge.   The 4.5 km chip trail around the <u>Cedar Hill Golf Course</u> is popular with hikers and joggers the year round. Phase II of the new <u>Cuthbert Holmes Park</u> is nearing completion. Phase I saw the construction of sturdy bridges over the Colquitz River. Phase II includes a large new parking lot accessed from Admirals Road just down from the Trans-Canada Highway. Many of the trails are surfaced with asphalt (wheelchair accessible); more to follow with Phase III. A map is available at the Municipal Hall.

<u>University of Victoria (see page ix):</u> In addition to the well-used joggers' "Chip Trip" around the perimeter of the campus, there are numerous other trails including the descent into Mystic Vale. The chip trail connects with the trails of Oak Bay's <u>Henderson Recreation Centre</u> (see page ix). Maps of the University are available at the Campus Housing office, and the Victorienteers have a trails map (scale 1:7500) available to non-members for $2.00 for a photo-copy.

<u>Uplands Park:</u> The Victorienteers have a trails map (scale 1:3000) available to non-members for $2.00 for a photo-copy. The Park itself, Cattle Point and the beach walk south to the Oak Bay Marina, provide great urban opportunities for bird-watching and for observing native flora.

<u>Victoria:</u> The City Parks Department (see page ix) has a Map and Guide brochure for its 44 parks. The booklet, **"Beacon Hill Park 1882 - 1982: A Brief History"** is also available for $1.50. The Victorienteers have a 5-colour map of Beacon Hill Park at a price of $3.00 for non-members. From the breakwater at Ogden Point, take the cliffside walk from Holland Point to Clover Point along Dallas Road. Adjacent to Beacon Hill Park, it offers magnificent views of the Olympic Mountains and the Strait

---

of Juan de Fuca. From Clover Point to historic Ross Bay Cemetery is a short walk along the esplanade.

Esquimalt: The Municipality's Parks and Recreation Commission (see page viii) has a glossy brochure with a map and description of the parks. Saxe Point Park, MacCauley Point Park and adjacent Fleming Beach offer spectacular views and many amenities. Highrock Park has a panoramic view of the surrounding area from the cairn lookout, and Kinsmen Gorge Park is just across the bridge from the Gorge Waterway. West Bay in Esquimalt (limited parking off Head Street) is the starting point of the as-yet unnamed waterfront walkway which stretches from Head Street to the Songhees development near the Johnson Street bridge in Victoria. The Provincial Capital Commission has cooperated with Esquimalt, Victoria, the B.C. Enterprise Corporation and the Songhees developers to complete the 3.5 km walkway. It is possible to gain access at several points along its length. By crossing the Johnson Street Bridge, one is able to walk along the Inner Harbour right around to Laurel Point on the other side, although detours are necessary at a couple of points to avoid the commercial transportation enterprises in the Harbour. The newest of these enterprises, the Victoria Harbour Ferry, makes a one-way loop trip possible. The tiny ferries make stops at the Songhees dock, on the Causeway in front of the Empress, at Fisherman's Wharf in front of Barb's Fish and Chips, and back at the West Bay Marina at the foot of Head Street. Summer, 1990, the ferries will run every 20 minutes from 10 a.m. to 10 p.m. Information is available at the kiosk on the Causeway, at the Tourist Information Bureau, and at West Bay Marina and R.V. Park, 453 Head St. (385-1831).

View Royal: The recently-incorporated Town of View Royal (see page ix) is home to Portage Park. The Park, with its archaeological sites, is currently being spruced up, and is to be found on the doorstep of the Town Hall.

Colwood: A map and inventory list of the City of Colwood's 21 parks is available for $2.00 from the Planning Department (see page viii). For the hiker, one of the best trails is the joggers' chip trail around the Juan de Fuca (CRD) Park. Fort Rodd Hill National Historic Park (see page viii) is open daily, 8 - 8 in summer. Nearby Esquimalt Lagoon is home to a bird sanctuary, and Royal Roads Military College (see page ix) opens its grounds (but not the buildings) to visitors daily, 8:30 - 5 in summer.

Metchosin (see page ix): The Municipality has been granted a licence of occupancy for Section 25, known variously as Metchosin Wilderness Park, Clapham Park and Hundred Acre Park (though Pooh would choose Hundred Acre Wood). Located off Rocky Point Road between Arden Road and Clapham Drive, its trails are shared by hikers and horseback riders. There are several viewpoints and its deep woods and small creeks offer an excellent shady hike for a hot day. If travelling by bus, take Metchosin #54 (infrequent service, none on Sundays and evenings) from Canwest Mall and get off on Rocky Point Road at Arden/Mathews/Lombard roads

---

intersection. Hike up Arden Road 1.9 km to trail access on left side of road below residence at 936 Arden Road. If hiking the Galloping Goose Corridor, hike from Kangaroo Road south along Rocky Point Road to Arden Road or from the trail along Lombard Road to Rocky Point Road and Arden Road. By car, proceed as follows: (1) from Rocky Point Road turn up Mathews/Arden Road and follow Arden Road 1.9 km, or (2) from Rocky Point Road turn right on Clapham Drive. Trail access is 0.5 km on right at large sign marked "Metchosin Park". There is no off-road parking; park along the roadside, easier at Clapham Drive. From Clapham Drive access follow the main trail, keeping right to viewpoint. Or, bearing left from access cross a bridge, straight ahead to a "T", each direction leading to viewpoints. Turning right after the bridge takes one to the Arden Road access. From Arden Road access, take the first left (and cross a bridge) and later a second bridge to a "T", left to the first-mentioned viewpoint or right to Clapham Drive access. Use bridges at your own risk, especially if on a horse.

Another new hike in Metchosin is the Seabluff Trail, donated by Geoff and B.H. Mitchell, long-time Metchosin residents. It is a short hike through open fields, along sea view bluffs (50 metres high, looking south to the Olympics), and through woods, skirting a small irrigation pond. Please do not disturb the sheep; dogs MUST be on a leash at all times; leave gates closed. Access is from Metchosin Road or William Head Road. By bus, take Metchosin #54 to Wootten Road or Parry Road. From Metchosin Road hike or drive down Wootten Road to gate (0.3 km); from William Head Road, proceed down Parry Road and turn left on Parry Cross Road to gate (0.6 km). On the site, follow the trail (road allowance) from Wootten Road to the bluffs, then turn right along the bluffs and then follow the trail back through woods, pass by the Parry Cross Road access and continue back to Wootten Road.

NOTES

Current road maps will be useful or even necessary adjuncts to these Revision Notes. References to the Victoria Natural History Society's **"The Naturalists's Guide to the Victoria Region"** can enhance your visit to any of the places we have described. Trail conditions and access information change constantly. The editorial committee welcomes any information or comments that would keep our books current and useful.

The Trails Information Society regularly donates from its profits toward suitable projects.

These Revision Notes were prepared by Susan Lawrence, who wishes to thank: John Harris, Jane Toms, Jane Waddell, and the many people in the public and private agencies who provided information.

NOTES

NOTES

NOTES

NOTES

HIKING TRAILS I
Victoria and Vicinity

includes area west to
Port Renfrew and north to
Oliphant Lake

compiled and edited by
Jane Waddell

Cover photo: Joyce Folbigg

Illustrations by courtesy of Judy Trousdell

First published as
HIKING TRAILS, Victoria and Southern Vancouver Island
in December 1972

Second printing January 1973
Third printing, February 1973
Fourth printing November 1973
Fifth printing February 1974
Revised, expanded and retitled November 1975
Revised February 1977
Revised April 1979
Revised and expanded October 1981
Tenth edition reprinted with revision notes © 1990

Published by
The Outdoor Club of Victoria Trails Information Society

Distributed by
Sono Nis Press, Victoria, B.C.

Maps by A. N. Fraser Drafting Services
Word Processing by Avalon Data Systems Ltd.
Printed by Morriss Printing Company Ltd., Victoria, B.C.

CONTENTS AND KEY TO MAPS

map   page

    About this booklet...   7

    Legend   9

    Hints & Cautions   10

(1) Coles Bay Regional Park   13

(2) Horth Hill Regional Park   14

(3) Sidney Spit Marine Provincial Park   16

(4) John Dean Provincial Park   18

(5) Willow Way, Central Saanich   22

(6) Mount Douglas Park   24

(7) Lochside Drive right-of-way south section   26

(8) Lochside Drive right-of-way north section;
     Island View Beach Regional Park   28

(9) Elk and Beaver Lakes Regional Park;
     Bear Hill Regional Park   32

(10) Colquitz River Linear Park   34

(11) Swan Lake Nature Sanctuary   37

(12) Mount Work Regional Park (includes
     McKenzie Bight and Durrance Lake)   38

(13) Lone Tree Hill Regional Park   42

(14) Thomas S. Francis/Freeman King Regional Park   43

(15) Thetis Lake Park   47

(16) Mill Hill Regional Park; abandoned CNR right-of-way
     (Atkins Road area)   50

(17) Goldstream Provincial Park; Mount Finlayson   52

(18) Witty's Lagoon Regional Park   56

(19) Devonian Regional Park   59

(20) East Sooke Regional Park   60

Abandoned Canadian National Railway right-of-way: 65

(21) Tillicum Mall to Highway Interchange   66

(22) Colwood Corners to Happy Valley Road   68

(23) Happy Valley Road to Matheson Lake   70

(24) Matheson Lake Provincial Park   **72**

(25) Roche Cove Regional Park   **74**

(26) Veitch Creek to Leechtown; Sooke Hills area   76

(27) Spectacle Lake Provincial Park; Oliphant Lake   80

**continued
overleaf**

Contents and Key to Maps, continued

Beach Access West of Sooke: 83

    French Beach Provincial Park
    Juan de Fuca Viewpoint
    Sandcut Creek Trail
    Jordan River Picnic Site
    China Beach Provincial Park
    Mystic Beach
(28)   Sombrio Beach

(29) Botanical Beach, Port Renfrew   86

The West Coast Trail   89

Club addresses; Useful Addresses and Information   90

Acknowledgements   92

Index

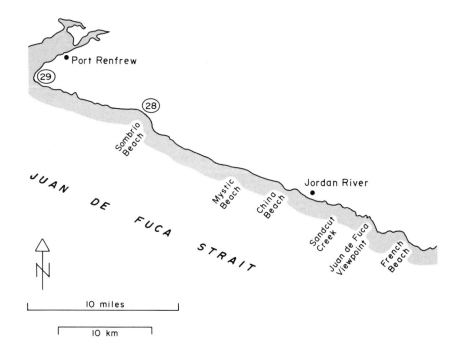

ABOUT THIS BOOKLET ...

In the last six years a great many changes have taken place in the Greater Victoria area and this tenth edition of our booklet contains much new information. In particular we are including for the first time three urban, or semi-urban walks -- the Lochside Drive right-of-way, the partly completed Colquitz River Linear Park and the abandoned Canadian National Railway right-of-way. With the growing population throughout Greater Victoria and the Saanich Peninsula the development of urban recreation of this sort becomes increasingly important. We hope this booklet will provide visitors and newcomers to this area, as well as longer time residents, with useful hiking information.

In the main we have omitted descriptions of the flora and fauna that you will find along the trails, emphasizing instead the access information you will need and trying as far as possible to give specific trail directions. The Capital Regional District and most of the other agencies have descriptive brochures and the natural history of the area is covered in the recently revised **"The Naturalist's Guide to the Victoria Region"** produced by the Victoria Natural History Society, plus the Sierra Club's **"Victoria in a Knapsack"**. More experienced hikers can explore other areas not included here which they can find for themselves (see useful addresses on page 90).

The Outdoor Club of Victoria was formed in 1942 by a group of Victorians interested in hiking together so they could share the companionship of others with similar interests and pool their knowledge of places to go. There are hikes every Sunday throughout the year and monthly evening meetings with entertainment programs. The current issue of the hiking schedule with telephone numbers as to who to contact is available at the public library. You will find details of other hiking clubs on page 90.

Please note that we cannot be held responsible for any discrepancies, inaccuracies or omissions in our maps and descriptions. Trails shown may be only approximate, as conditions vary constantly. Hikers always travel at their own risk and it is up to the individual hiker to check current conditions by enquiring at offices of the appropriate authority or by asking local residents and officials. It is particularly important to do so before setting out on the longer trips.

We have produced two other booklets covering other areas of Vancouver Island and these also are revised from time to time (see back cover for details).

The public's continued response to our voluntary project is most rewarding and I want to thank all those who have contributed to its success. Some of their names are listed in this booklet, but there have been many other helpers also. I am very grateful to Joyce Folbigg, John Harris, John Pinder-Moss and Jane Toms for their editorial assistance; also to the members of our non-profit society and to our voluntary salespersons who faithfully give their support.

December, 1986   **Jane Waddell**
                                  Editor

LEGEND

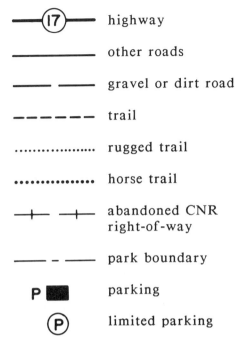

highway

other roads

gravel or dirt road

trail

rugged trail

horse trail

abandoned CNR
right-of-way

park boundary

P ▮ parking

Ⓟ limited parking

Inset diagrams show how the maps
inter-relate.

**Note that maps are not all at the
same scale.**

Picnic tables and toilet facilities
are not shown on maps. These are
termed "parks facilities" and will
usually be found near the main
parking area.

HINTS AND CAUTIONS

Trails. While only some of the well established, better known trails are described here, they may lead to other opportunities which can be pursued by the more experienced and hardy. Most of the trails are footpaths; a few can be used by horses where permitted by park regulations. Riders should avoid disturbing the full width of trails at muddy spots. Trail bikes are prohibited in all parks.

Good clothing is essential. All these trails can be hiked in good walking shoes or even runners, but you will be better off in comfortable boots as trails can sometimes be muddy or steep in places. A small packsack is a good way to carry lunch, maps, camera, extra sweater, rainwear, swim suit, insect repellant and any essential First Aid requirements. Articles placed in a plastic garbage bag inside your packsack will remain dry in the wettest weather.

Do not litter the trails. Don't drop gum wrappers, orange peel, lunch bags or soft drink cans. Carry them out in your packsack.

Please be careful with fires, especially during dry weather. Fires are not permitted in many areas or permits may be necessary from local fire departments. Above all, put fires thoroughly out! Clear an area free from flammable materials around your fire to a distance of at least one metre and do not establish a fire within at least three metres of any log, bush or tree. Pour water on the fire afterwards and sort through the ashes with your bare hands to be certain there are no hot spots left which could flame up again. Smoke only at rest stops ... never when walking ... be sure that cigarettes and matches are completely extinguished.

Maps and compass. Those who would explore off the trails may find topographical maps useful; these can be obtained from the B.C. provincial government in Victoria. For details of street and mailing addresses see page 90. Maps are also available through the Government Agent in major towns (i.e., Duncan).

An aerial photograph is sometimes a useful companion to a map and can be obtained from the above offices. These often show details that are not visible on maps and may be more up to date. Other maps may be obtained from parks agencies (i.e., provincial parks and regional district offices); and from logging companies (see page 90, 91). A compass and knowledge of how to use it is also useful, since one loses direction easily and even on a trail it can be difficult to tell which way to turn. An altimeter too is often very useful in obscure weather.

Contour lines on maps show the roughness of the terrain; the closer together the lines, the steeper the hillsides.

To prevent your map (or booklet) from becoming damaged on the trail, it is a good idea to carry with you only a photocopy of the area in which you are interested.

Do not hike alone. The greatest danger is probably from slipping on loose rocks on moss-covered hillsides, or on logs. The wise hiker travels with a friend in case of an accident. A whistle is useful for communication if separated. If lost, logging roads and streams generally lead out if one follows them downhill. Cross-country scrambling is difficult, so stay on trails unless absolutely certain where you are going. Leave information on your plans, including the expected time of return, with someone who is reliable and remember that searches in our rough terrain are difficult and expensive.

Hunting season. Be aware of the danger of being mistaken for a wild animal during hunting season and wear bright clothing. Carry a whistle or horn to warn hunters of your presence. Avoid heavily hunted areas.

Traversing private property. Ask permission. Close gates if found closed; leave them open if found open. Respect logging company signs; in this area most of their holdings are owned by them, not leased public lands. Do not damage equipment and report those you see doing so. Be considerate of your fellow hiker. Take nothing and leave nothing.

Flowers and plants. Particularly in parks where it is illegal, but in other places too, leave wild flowers where you find them. Unlike garden varieties they seldom last long when picked and uprooted specimens rarely can be transplanted to city gardens.

Mosquitoes and other flying pests. These can be a nuisance and you may need to carry a repellant. Wasps should be avoided; they nest in the ground and in bag-like nests in trees. Poisonous plants and dangerous animals (bears) are seldom a problem. Poison oak is rare. While there are many edible plants, there are some poisonous ones. Eat wild mushrooms only if certain they are edible. The stinging nettle and devil's club may be encountered on Southern Vancouver Island but contact with these is only irritating.

Do not chop "blazes" into trees. They are unsightly and lead to infection by a variety of insects and diseases. If for some reason you wish to mark a trail with plastic tape, keep use of it to a minimum as it deteriorates slowly. A more temporary marker is toilet paper, easily seen and useful in any packsack.

John W.E. Harris

MAP 1 - COLES BAY REGIONAL PARK

Coles Bay Park (3.6 hectares), about 23 km from Victoria via Highway 17 and West Saanich Road, is signposted at Ardmore Drive and at Inverness Road to the park entrance. A 10-minute walk by either trail from the parking lot brings one to the rocky, pebble and mud beach which is best at low tide.

A CRD brochure is available.

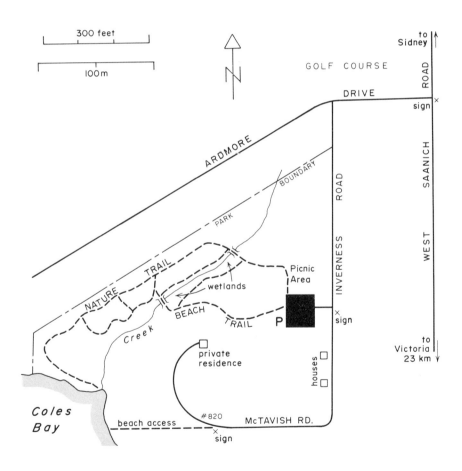

14

MAP 2
HORTH HILL REGIONAL PARK

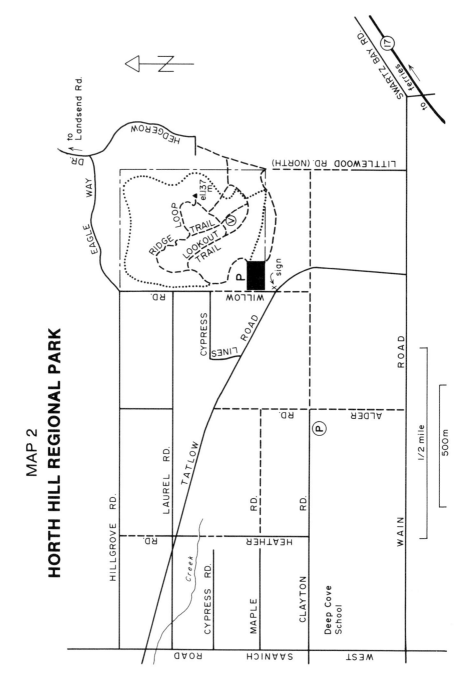

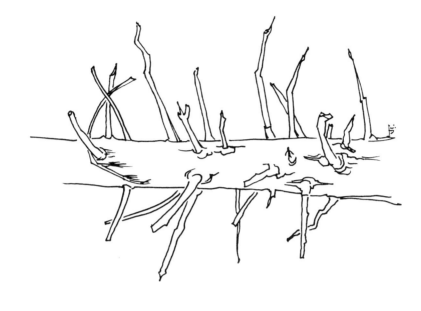

HORTH HILL REGIONAL PARK AND AREA

Travelling to Swartz Bay from Victoria, just before the ferry terminal turn left at the traffic lights onto Wain Road, then right onto Tatlow Road to the signposted parking lot of Horth Hill Regional Park (20 hectares)--about 40 minutes drive from Victoria, 30 km. From the parking lot the northern trail through the forest soon divides into the Lookout Trail and the steeper Ridge Trail. Both lead to fine overviews of the islands around Sidney and the Saanich Inlet, though the bushy summit has no viewpoint.

Look for the ladyslipper orchid along the trail. Horse trails intersect the hiking and other minor trails. Your walk may be extended by following any of the unopened road rights-of-way shown on the map.

A CRD brochure is available; also a leaflet by the Sunset Riding Club and District of North Saanich (phone 656-0781) showing their unopened road rights-of-way for hikers and horsemen.

MAP 3 - SIDNEY SPIT MARINE PROVINCIAL PARK

For location see general map on Table of Contents. Access is by boat or kayak only--distance from Sidney about 5 km. A ferry runs during the summer months from the foot of Beacon Avenue. During 1986 the capacity of the one boat making the 25-minute trip was 21 passengers and it is hoped that in 1987 there will be two ferries. For information phone 385-6392.

The 400-hectare park has full marine parks facilities including wilderness, walk-in campgrounds. No camping is permitted on the Claw.

At low tide one can hike for miles along the Spit or Claw, with year-round opportunities for the enjoyment of hikers, naturalists and birdwatchers.

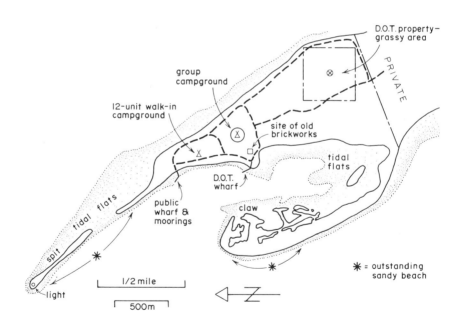

The portion south of the lagoon is privately owned with a herd of fallow deer which frequently wander into the park.

Caution! Be careful with fires. The forest is very dry in summer and fire poses a great hazard.

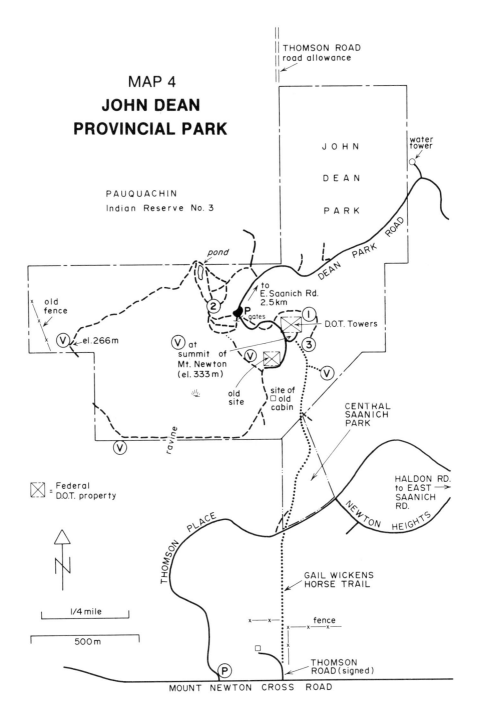

MAP 4
JOHN DEAN
PROVINCIAL PARK

THOMSON ROAD
road allowance

J O H N

D E A N

P A R K

water
tower

PAUQUACHIN
Indian Reserve No. 3

DEAN PARK ROAD

pond

to
E. Saanich Rd.
2.5 km

old
fence

② P gates

① D.O.T. Towers

Ⓥ el. 266 m

③

Ⓥ at
summit of
Mt. Newton
(el. 333 m)

Ⓥ

Ⓥ

old
site

site of
old
cabin

CENTRAL
SAANICH
PARK

Ⓥ

ravine

⊠ = Federal
  D.O.T. property

HALDON RD.
to EAST
SAANICH
RD.

NEWTON HEIGHTS

THOMSON PLACE

N

GAIL WICKENS
HORSE TRAIL

1/4 mile

500 m

fence
x — x   x — x

THOMSON
ROAD (signed)

Ⓟ

MOUNT NEWTON CROSS ROAD

From Victoria, access to John Dean Park by car is by Highway 17 and East Saanich Road. At Gulf View Picnic Site turn left onto Dean Park Road which passes through Dean Park Estate and on to the parking lot. Driving time is about 40 minutes -- 23 km. Horses are permitted in the park but no camping is allowed. Dogs must be on a leash. See map for the following notes:

(1) A five-minute walk up on the paved road will bring you to the federal DOT radar towers. From the clearing by this site there are good views over the Gulf Islands and many wild flowers in season.

(2) Parks facilities are provided here, including fire pits and a water pump. Trails north lead to a beautiful pond at the park boundary, with salamanders, frogs and water lilies. Several trails lead back to the parking lot. A circle trip around these trails takes about 45 minutes. If the hike westward up to the viewpoint over the Saanich Inlet is included, add another 20 minutes.

(3) From the paved road a trail leads down southward, which becomes the Gail Wickens Horse Trail. This crosses Thomson Place between the houses numbered 8233 and 8257 (parking possible here only on shoulder of road) and continues along Thomson Road unopened road right-of-way to Mount Newton Cross Road (parking space here for only one car). It is fairly steep in parts. The return trip takes about 90 minutes.

John Dean was a bachelor and an individualist with a good eye for real estate. He was considered crusty but another side of his nature was revealed after he was persuaded to let the Sidney Boy Scout Troop hold a campout on his property up on Mount Newton. He had feared vandalism, but to his amazement the Scouts -- under the leadership of Skipper Freeman King -- left the place cleaner than they had found it. From now on John Dean became an ardent supporter of the Boy Scout movement and showed a warm enthusiasm for the young. In 1921 at the age of 70 he donated 32 hectares of his property to the province for parkland. Various additions of land have increased the park's size to 155 hectares. During the 1930s federally funded relief crews constructed what we now call Dean Park Road (originally a fire access road). Skipper Freeman King was the crew foreman who supervised the construction of trails and of the picnic area sited in a grove of very large trees. The steps, the stone walling, the lily pond which was formerly a swamp and the remains of a tea-house are all still there.

John Dean died at the age of 92, having written his own epi-taph: "It's a rotten world, artful politicians are its bane..." His grave is in Ross Bay Cemetery beside a large monkey puzzle tree and is worth a visit.

By walking eastwards along Mount Newton X Road from Thomson Road to Saanichton School, a link can be made via Malcolm and Hovey Roads to the Willow Way circuit (see Map 5).

The recently formed Friends of John Dean Park (phone 656-9276) will actively cooperate with the B.C. Parks and Outdoor Recreation Division and all users of the park to develop and maintain it.

22

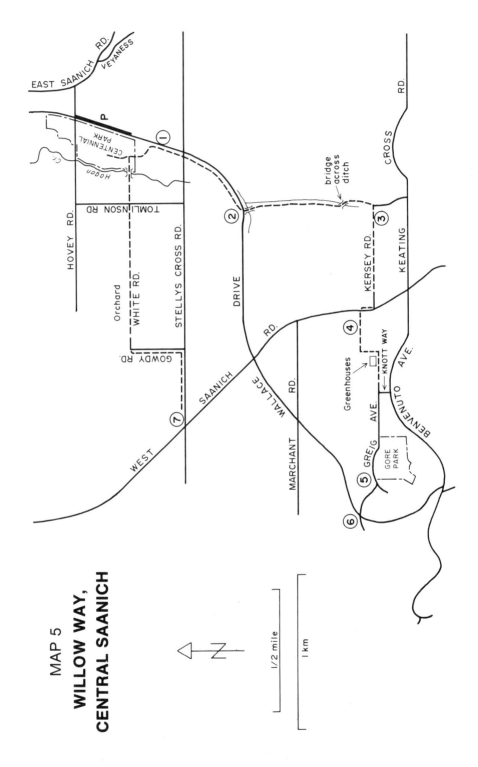

MAP 5
WILLOW WAY,
CENTRAL SAANICH

1/2 mile

1 km

WILLOW WAY, CENTRAL SAANICH

Our map shows a pleasant 10-km circle route for cyclists, hikers and horsemen through narrow roads (where care is necessary to avoid cars) and along unopened road rights-of-way beside fences, in the flat or rolling farmlands of Central Saanich. Car access from Victoria is by Highway #17, East Saanich Road and Hovey Road to Centennial Park (about 18 km—a half hour drive); excellent parking and parks facilities.

(1) From Centennial Park follow the broad shoulder of the road south to a foot-bridge.

(2) Follow right-of-way S along west side of ditch switching to east side.

(3) Follow Kersey Road (clearly evident at houses) to West Saanich Road.

(4) Trail here is rough and grassy. Continue past greenhouses to Greig Avenue.

(5) Visit Gore Nature Park, very pretty and unspoiled. Limited parking here.

(6) Via Wallace Drive and West Saanich Road go NE, then NW.

(7) At Stelly's Cross Road turn E to Gowdy Road and then on to White Road. The right-of-way runs along the S edge of the orchard, crosses Tomlinson Road and Hagan Creek, returning to Centennial Park.

Cautions: Be careful of private property, including fences and livestock. Keep off planted fields, especially if on horseback. Keep dogs under control. Please do not smoke, due to fire hazard. No motor cycles please.

A recreational leaflet is available from Central Saanich Municipality.

MAP 6 - MOUNT DOUGLAS PARK

Mount Douglas Park (148 hectares) is jointly funded by the City of Victoria and Saanich Municipality. It is 8 km NE of Victoria via Hillside, or Shelbourne, accessible by car or #28 bus--about 20 minutes' drive by car. Another 1.5 km brings you to the summit parking lot and to several very fine viewpoints.

Excellent parking space and picnicking facilities are to be found at (1) from where a trail leads down to the beach. Several trails are signposted from Cordova Bay Road from which you can plan some good hiking. The Irvine Trail leads up to a viewpoint over Cordova Bay.

(2) No parking is allowed along Cordova Bay Road here. About 100 m beyond the quarry find the Merriman Trail (signed) and follow it to the summit--well defined and easy hiking in the lower section, but somewhat indistinct and steeper at the summit. The Birch Trail offers the easiest ascent to the summit with a viewpoint of its own near the top.

(3) The Norn Trail is well defined and provides easy walking on fairly level ground. It roughly parallels Cordova Bay Road passing through tall timber; other trails lead back to (1) or (3)

(4) There is very limited parking space for cars along Blenkinsop Road. Between houses #4351 and #4411 find the Mercer Trail (signed) and then pick up the Munson Trail which takes you to the old mine workings. You can then climb up over a rocky ridge with Garry Oak and low bush and in spring time will find here lovely flowers. Or go north from the mine on the Whittaker Trail and make side trips to excellent views.

(5) Note the blowdown here caused by a typhoon in the mid-1950s (started in Guam).

(6) and (7) Very limited car parking. The lower sections of these trails offer pleasant walking through tall timber. The Summit Trail is steep and in places rocky.

No camping is permitted. In the picnic area no horses are permitted at any time; dogs are allowed here from September to April only.

ROAD

BLENKINSOP

PEARCE CRESC.

Ⓟ

LOHBRUNNER

MUNSON

(4)

MERCER

BLENKINSOP

ROAD

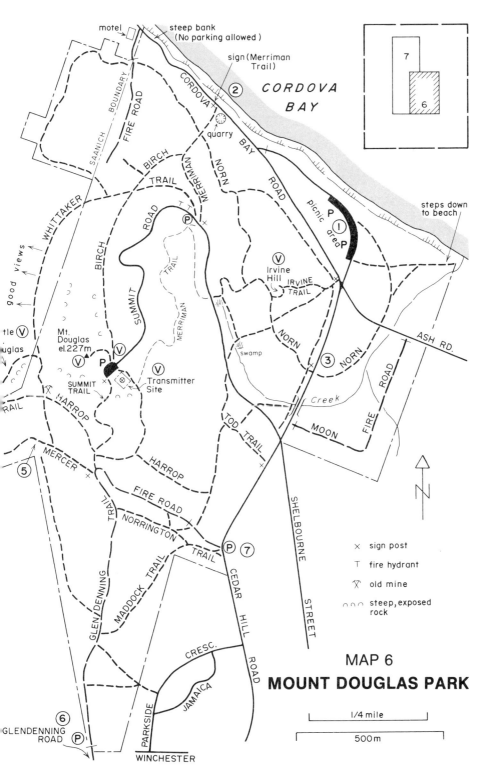

MAP 6
MOUNT DOUGLAS PARK

| 1/4 mile |
| 500 m |

× sign post

T fire hydrant

⚒ old mine

⌒⌒⌒ steep, exposed rock

CORDOVA BAY

steep bank
(No parking allowed)

sign (Merriman Trail)

quarry

steps down
to beach

picnic area

Irvine Hill

IRVINE TRAIL

swamp

Creek

Mt. Douglas
el. 227m

SUMMIT TRAIL

Transmitter Site

good views

WHITTAKER TRAIL

BIRCH TRAIL

BIRCH ROAD

MERRIMAN TRAIL

NORN ROAD

CORDOVA BAY ROAD

SAANICH BOUNDARY

FIRE ROAD

SUMMIT TRAIL

MERRIMAN TRAIL

NORN TRAIL

NORN

MOON

ASH RD.

FIRE ROAD

HARROP

HARROP FIRE ROAD

MERCER TRAIL

NORRINGTON TRAIL

GLENDENNING TRAIL

MADDOCK TRAIL

TOD TRAIL

CEDAR HILL ROAD

SHELBOURNE STREET

CRESC.

JAMAICA

PARKSIDE

WINCHESTER

GLENDENNING ROAD

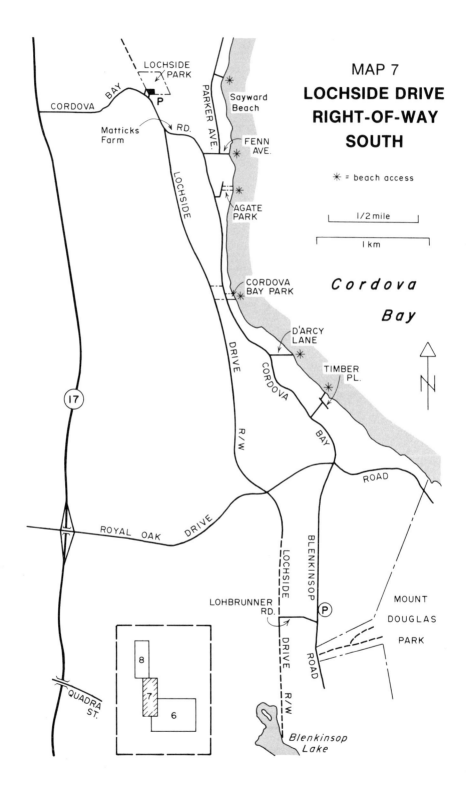

MAP 7
**LOCHSIDE DRIVE
RIGHT-OF-WAY
SOUTH**

＊ = beach access

1/2 mile

1 km

Cordova

Bay

LOCHSIDE
PARK

P

CORDOVA   BAY

Matticks
Farm

RD.

PARKER AVE.

Sayward
Beach

＊

FENN
AVE.
＊

LOCHSIDE

＊
AGATE
PARK

CORDOVA
BAY PARK
＊

D'ARCY
LANE
＊

DRIVE

CORDOVA

TIMBER
PL.
＊

N

17

R/W

BAY

ROAD

ROYAL   OAK   DRIVE

BLENKINSOP

LOCHSIDE

LOHBRUNNER
RD.

P

MOUNT

DOUGLAS

PARK

DRIVE

ROAD

QUADRA
ST.

8

7

6

R/W

*Blenkinsop
Lake*

The Lochside Drive right-of-way (the roadbed of the old C.N.Railway) roughly parallels Highway #17, passing through Saanich and Central Saanich and a pleasant 10-km walk one way along it is possible.

The right-of-way is in part residentially developed and partly through open farmland. Whether these open sections will remain undeveloped is unknown (1986), but it is hoped that a linear park will maintain the recreational use of the right-of-way. A map of the Greater Victoria area would be a useful adjunct to this information.

Map 7 - Lochside Drive right-of-way, south

From Blenkinsop Road at Lohbrunner Road the distance to Lochside Park is 4.5 km. Parking is limited at Blenkinsop Road but good at Lochside Park. This south section of the walk is to a greater extent residentially developed. Note that from Lohbrunner Road the right-of-way continues south to Blenkinsop Lake (a 10-minute walk) to the naturalists' bird blind. Note also that easy access can be made from Lohbrunner Road to the Mercer Trail in Mount Douglas Park.

The following beach accesses from Cordova Bay Road, provided by the Saanich Municipality, are shown on this map:

* Timber Place (off Timber Road). Some parking space available. Steps down to beach.

* D'Arcy Lane. No parking in the lane, but limited parking on shoulder of Cordova Bay Road.

   Both the above can be accessed at low to medium tide.

* Cordova Bay Park, beside grocery store. Good parking and easy beach access at all times.

* #5113 - McMorran's Restaurant. Parking and easy access at all times.

* Agate Beach off Agate Avenue. Excellent parking and access at all times.

* Fenn Avenue. Minimal parking. Steps down to beach.

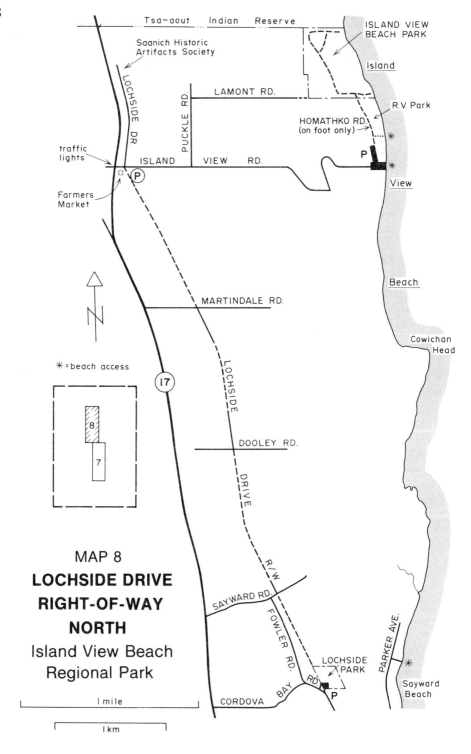

Tsa-aout   Indian   Reserve

ISLAND VIEW
BEACH PARK

Saanich Historic
Artifacts Society

Island

LOCHSIDE DR.

PUCKLE RD.

LAMONT RD.

R.V. Park

HOMATHKO RD.
(on foot only)

traffic
lights

P

ISLAND   VIEW   RD.

P

View

Farmers
Market

Beach

N

MARTINDALE RD.

Cowichan
Head

* = beach access

17

LOCHSIDE

8

7

DOOLEY RD.

DRIVE

MAP 8
**LOCHSIDE DRIVE
RIGHT-OF-WAY
NORTH**
Island View Beach
Regional Park

R/W

SAYWARD RD.

FOWLER RD.

PARKER AVE.

LOCHSIDE
PARK

RD.

P

Sayward
Beach

1 mile

CORDOVA   BAY

1 km

* Parker Avenue (off Fenn Avenue). Just beyond #5397 there is a large parking lot with steps down to the beach. Useful access at low tide.

Map 8 - Lochside Drive right-of-way, north

From Lochside Park to Highway #17 at Island View Road the distance is 5.5 km. From here the right-of-way continues to the Saanich Historical Artifacts Society grounds (open in summer 10 am to 4 pm). Currently (1986) this north section of the right-of-way is almost entirely through open farmland. This makes a very pleasant walk, but note that after heavy rain there can be some muddy sections.

Island View Beach Regional Park - also on Map 8

From Victoria on Highway #17 drive about 16 km and turn right onto Island View Road at traffic lights. Another 2.5 km brings you to the large CRD parking lot and to the beach. Access to Island View Beach Park (25.4 hectares) can be made along the beach at all times, or by Homathko Road (on foot only). The park is undeveloped, with some old trails, the occasional picnic table, unique sand dunes and a natural berm. Please treat these natural features with great respect as the ecology is very fragile.

From a hiker's point of view this is the best and closest beach to Victoria, with a view across Haro Strait to the San Juan

Islands, Sidney Spit and Mount Baker. Note that swimming is not recommended on account of strong currents. A CRD brochure is available.

A roughly marked right-of-way from Lamont Road to the south boundary of the park exists (not suitable for horses).

On a minus low tide, a 10-km one-way beach walk is possible from Island View Beach to Mount Douglas Park with minimal rock scrambling. This can be another very pleasant walk.

Beach accesses are shown on our map with an asterisk.

See also **"Gateway To Victoria's Beaches"** by Barbara Chapman (1976), in libraries only.

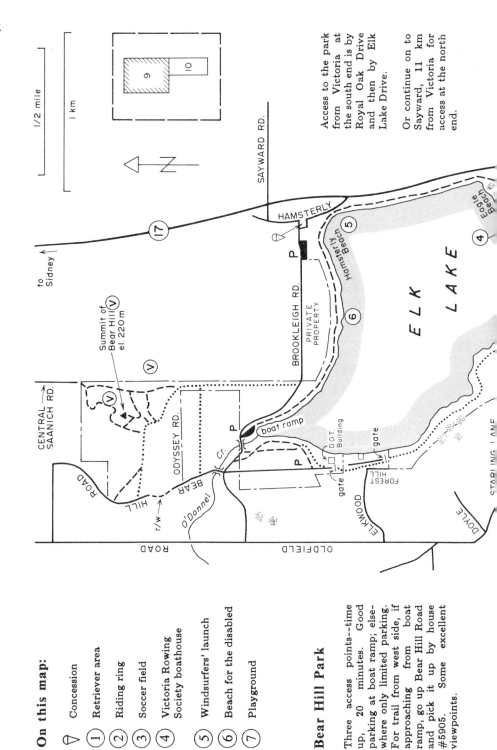

On this map:

⚑ Concession

① Retriever area

② Riding ring

③ Soccer field

④ Victoria Rowing Society boathouse

⑤ Windsurfers' launch

⑥ Beach for the disabled

⑦ Playground

Bear Hill Park

Three access points--time up, 20 minutes. Good parking at boat ramp; else-where only limited parking. For trail from west side, if approaching from boat ramp, go up Bear Hill Road and pick it up by house #5905. Some excellent viewpoints.

Access to the park from Victoria at the south end is by Royal Oak Drive and then by Elk Lake Drive.

Or continue on to Sayward, 11 km from Victoria for access at the north end.

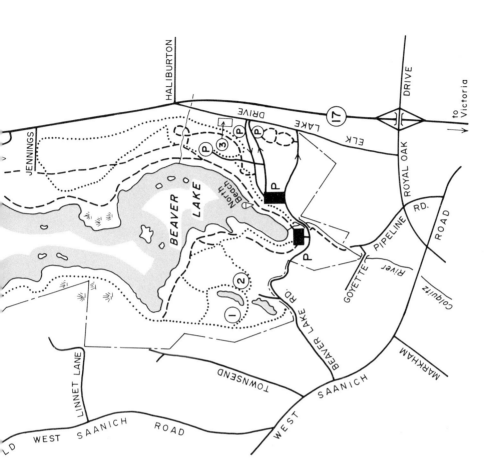

In the early 1900s the lakes were the water supply for the City of Victoria. The old filter beds at the south end of Beaver Lake are now filled in to make the big parking lot.

On the west side of the lakes the trail often follows the bed of the old Victoria and Sidney railroad.

A walk around the two lakes is about 9 km on a level trail.

Horse trails are clearly marked with red horse and rider markers. Hiking trails are marked with yellow markers.

There are parks facilities throughout the park. A CRD brochure is available.

MAP 9

ELK AND BEAVER LAKES REGIONAL PARK

BEAR HILL REGIONAL PARK

34

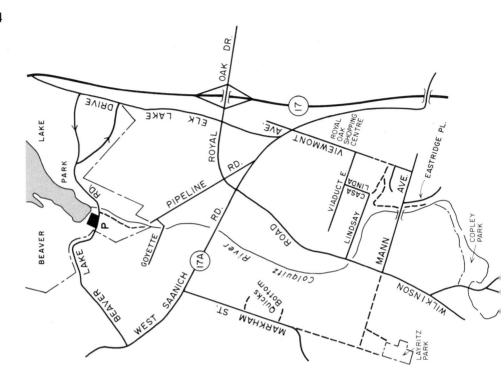

MAP 10 - COLQUITZ RIVER LINEAR PARK
(partly completed)

Saanich Municipality, funded by the Provincial Capital Commission, plans to develop a park and trail system from Portage Inlet to Beaver Lake. Part of this has already been developed and elaborately landscaped. The rest will be completed as opportunity arises. It is currently possible to walk about 8 km from the Tillicum Mall, past the Pacific Forestry Centre on Burnside Road, to Beaver Lake on trails, unopened road rights-of-way and some roads.

Colquitz River Park South (see Map 21) starts from the Tillicum Mall from where one can follow the Colquitz River Trail N going under Highway #1 and passing the Pacific Forestry Centre to the left. Or one can park in the visitor parking at the Forestry Centre and hike down through fields and woods to the creekside trail. Continue north under the McKenzie Avenue Bridge and on to Colquitz River Park North and if you so wish, into Hyacinth Park.

To continue the walk on to Beaver Lake, until this section of the linear park is developed, turn NE onto Marigold Road, then left onto Carey Road and left again onto Roy Road (thus avoiding Panama Flats, a maze of undeveloped trails, usually flooded in winter and spring). Turn right onto the Grange unopened road right-of-way coming out onto Carey and on to Copley Park. Follow the trail generally eastwards, then N (creek on your right), then cross another bridge to Mann Avenue. Turn left (W) and continue on Mann Avenue (crossing Wilkinson Road), through a yellow barricade still following Mann unopened road right-of-way and through some trees. Layritz Park is on your left. At the far

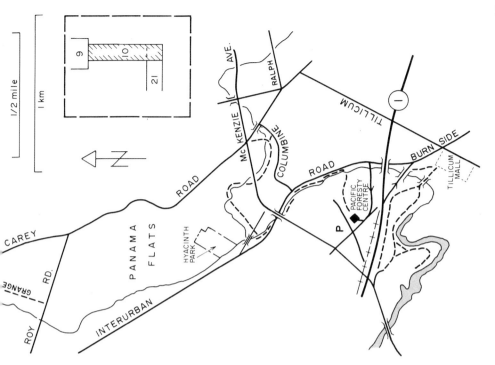

side of the playing field turn N onto Markham Street to West Saanich Road. (If doing this walk in reverse, going S on Markham Street pass signposted trail to Quicks Bottom--an observation area for naturalists--and at a curve in the road find right-of-way signposted S to Layritz Park. Beside toilets--usually locked--turn left onto trail through yellow barricade, then right onto Mann unopened road right-of-way to the next yellow barricade and so on ... A return loop to Beaver Lake can be made by picking up the trail following along the Colquitz River north from #764 Mann Avenue, then through fields to Viewmont Avenue to Royal Oak Shopping Centre, and so back to Pipeline Road and thence to Beaver Lake.)

Continuing N from Markham Street, turn left on West Saanich Road, right onto Beaver Lake Road and into Beaver Lake Park to the large south parking lot.

Note:

Saanich Municipality will in time acquire properties along the river to complete their linear park, making these detours by road unnecessary.

From Colquitz River Park North, about 50 metres E of Marigold Road a trail goes NE which becomes an excellent chip trail crossing Swan Creek twice, then passing under McKenzie Avenue and so on to Columbine Way. By walking on Carey and Ralph Roads one can reach Swan Lake Nature Sanctuary, but this involves crossing busy roads.

From the Pacific Forestry Centre on Burnside Road the walk can be extended westward (see page 66).

MAP 11 - SWAN LAKE

The Swan Lake Christmas Hill Nature Sanctuary comprises 46 hectares of lake, marsh, fields and thickets near Douglas Street and McKenzie Avenue. The Sanctuary, managed by a non-profit Society, is a wildlife refuge, an environmental education centre and a natural area for people to enjoy.

The grounds, open year round, can be explored on a 3-km network of trails and floating walkways, but during periods of heavy rainfall it is advisable to call ahead; phone 479-0211. The Nature House itself is closed during December and January. A new Nature House is proposed. A pamphlet is available on request. Public programs are held occasionally and groups are encouraged to pre-arrange conducted programs.

MOUNT WORK REGIONAL PARK

The park (415 hectares) is located in the SW part of the Saanich Peninsula, about 22.5 km NW of Victoria. It includes the McKenzie Bight coastline, Durrance Lake and Mount Work. A CRD brochure is available.

Access from Victoria is by Highway #17 - West Saanich Road - Wallace Drive (follow signs to Heal's Rifle Range) - and Durrance Road, about 45 minutes by car. Two signposted parking areas beyond Durrance Lake give access to trails to all areas of the park. At the south end of the park the Corry Road trailhead is signposted at the small parking lot on Munns Road. This can be accessed by either Prospect Lake Road and Munns Road, about 6 km beyond the Francis Park Nature House on a winding road; or from Highway #1 - Millstream Road - Millstream Lake Road - Munns Road.

Durrance Lake is a good place to swim and a pretty trail follows around its shoreline on the south side. From the parking lot at the head of the McKenzie Bight trail to the top of Mount Work allow one hour. It is fairly steep in parts with open hiking areas and beautiful views. At the first lookout take time for views of Central Saanich and the islands in Haro Strait. From the summit overlook there are pleasant views over to Finlayson Arm and the Malahat. From the Corry Road parking lot to the top of Mount Work allow 50 minutes--good views along the way.

The McKenzie Bight trails are signposted and provide short, pleasant hikes with good picnic spots at the Bight. Time down - 20 minutes. The Cascade Falls can be spectacular, particularly as seen from the trail on the west side of the creek.

A 21-metre parkland strip has been dedicated extending NE from the Bight up to Mark Lane, also SW to Elbow Point. You can follow an old road (4-wheel drive only) to Mark Lane. Westward from the Bight a rough trail follows the coastline to Elbow Point to a fine view up the Inlet (4 km one way).

Note:

* There are many old logging roads in the park as shown on our map.

* In the Mount Work area hikers are advised to stay on the trails as in foggy weather it is easy to become disoriented.

* No camping or fires are allowed in the park.

* Carry your own water. **Do not litter the park**.

* The addition of Todd Creek/Inlet to the park is proposed.

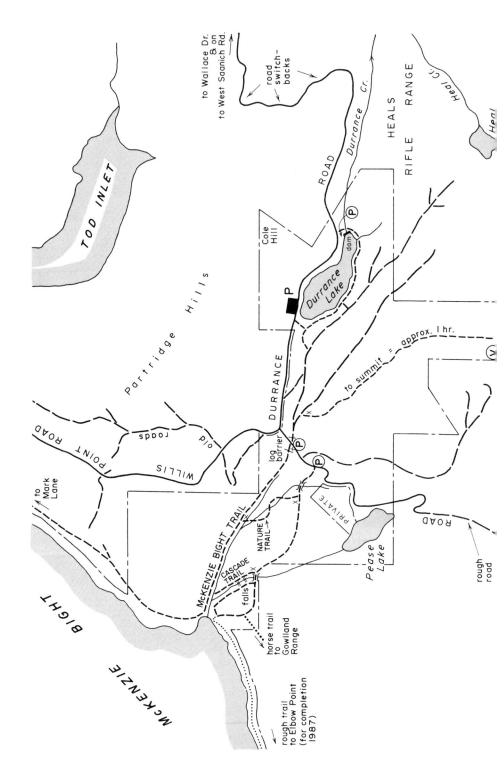

41

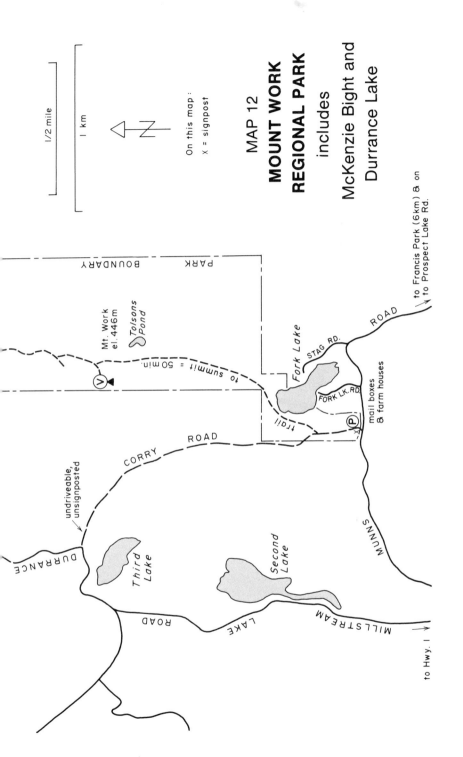

MAP 12
**MOUNT WORK
REGIONAL PARK**
includes
McKenzie Bight and
Durrance Lake

On this map :
x = signpost

1/2 mile

1 km

to Francis Park (6km) & on
to Prospect Lake Rd.

PARK BOUNDARY

Mt. Work
el. 446m

Tolsons
Pond

to summit = 50 min.

Fork Lake

STAG RD.

ROAD

FORK LK. RD.

mail boxes
& farm houses

P

trail

CORRY ROAD

undriveable,
unsignposted

DURRANCE

Third
Lake

Second
Lake

MUNNS

ROAD

LAKE

MILLSTREAM

to Hwy. I

MAP 13 - LONE TREE HILL REGIONAL PARK

On Highway #1 turn north at Millstream Road. Follow for 5.5 km, then take left fork (signposted to the park) and continue on Millstream Road; another 3 km to the park. Limited parking on shoulder of road only. No parks facilities (1986).

The trail climbs steadily up to an excellent view of the Malahat, the Gowlland Range, Victoria and the Olympic Mountains. The lone tree at the summit, gnarled and stunted, is now a heritage tree. The open slopes invite one to descend over them, but please resist this temptation as the 31-hectare park's ecology is very delicate. A CRD brochure is available.

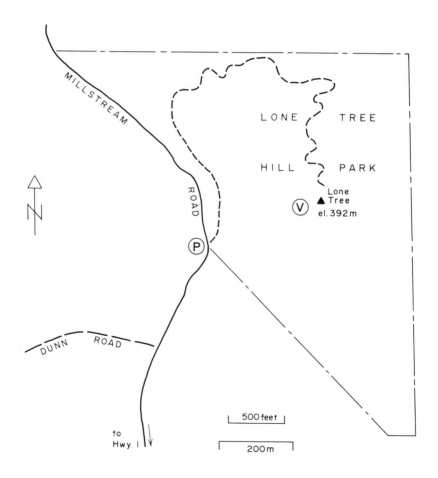

THOMAS FRANCIS/
FREEMAN KING REGIONAL PARK

This is bounded approximately by Prospect Lake Road to the east and adjoins Thetis Lake Park on the west. Access: (1) from Victoria about 7 km NW via McKenzie, Burnside, Prospect Lake Road and Munns Road; (2) follow Prospect Lake Road about 6 km generally south from its intersection with West Saanich Road just north of the Astrophysical Observatory, then right onto Munns Road.

Francis Park was donated by the late Thomas Francis in 1960 (43 hectares) and to this has been added Freeman King Park (20 hectares) named in honour of a local naturalist, the late "Skipper" Freeman King, which together with other acquisitions brings the present total to 91 hectares.

Within this area can be found a great variety of terrain--rain forest, rocky ledges, woodland meadows and swamp. Trails were cut by members of the Junior Natural History Society under the leadership of Freeman King. Over the years these have been modified and renamed and are well signposted and marked with different colours. Each would take about 30 minutes to walk and the signs along the way provide self-guided nature tours. Most trails lead back to the Nature House which contains posters and displays. Parks facilities will be found near the Nature House.

An important feature of Francis Park is the boardwalk named for Mrs. Freeman King. This was especially constructed in 1981 so that the handicapped may also enjoy the park from a wheelchair. It is complete with its own picnic table and shelter. There is also a special washroom facility for the disabled behind the Nature House.

A CRD brochure is available. In addition, the Victoria Natural History Society funds part-time naturalists. To book a nature walk or reserve a wheelchair phone 478-3344.

No horses or vehicles (including bicycles) are allowed on trails. All dogs must be on leash.

44

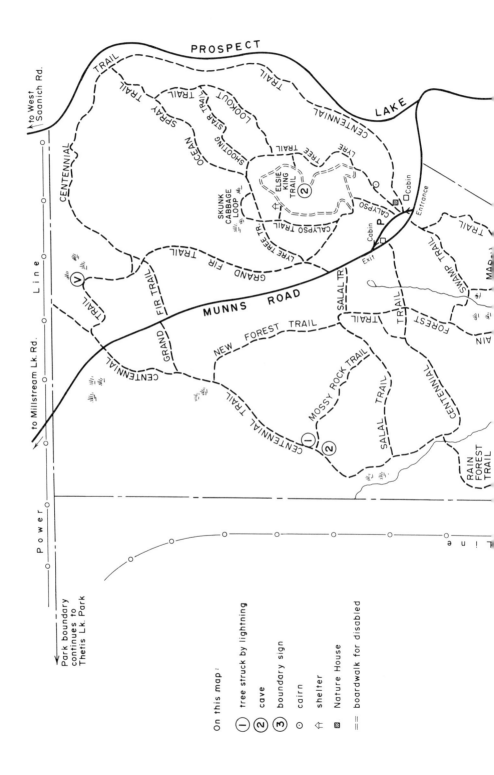

On this map:

① tree struck by lightning

② cave

③ boundary sign

◉ cairn

⛺ shelter

▨ Nature House

= boardwalk for disabled

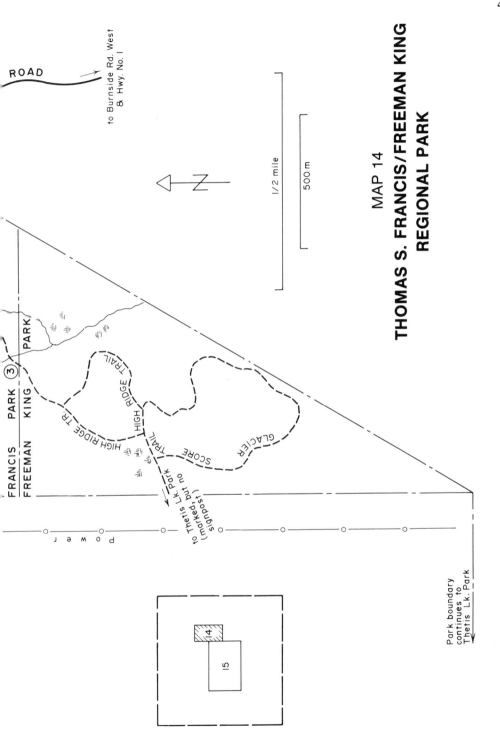

ROAD

to Burnside Rd. West
& Hwy. No. I

N

1/2 mile

500 m

MAP 14

THOMAS S. FRANCIS/FREEMAN KING
REGIONAL PARK

FRANCIS   PARK ③

FREEMAN KING   PARK

HIGH RIDGE TR.

HIGH RIDGE TRAIL

SCORE TRAIL

GLACIER

to Thetis Lk. Park
(marked, but no
signpost)

Power

14

15

Park boundary
continues to
Thetis Lk. Park

About 9 km on Highway #1 brings you to the main parking area of Thetis Lake Park (661 hectares). From late May to late August paid parking here generates funds for the maintenance of the park. Elsewhere there is limited parking only. The park is spectacular for its many wild flowers in spring, outcrops of moss-covered bedrock, arbutus, Garry Oak and Douglas Fir. Parks facilities include a swimming area. Power boats and camping are prohibited.

For a short one-hour hike follow the trail just east of Lower Lake to the bridge at the junction of the lakes, then the fire road back to the parking area. Allow two hours to hike around both lakes. The high trail east of Lower Lake leads up onto Seymour Hill to a cairn and good viewpoint.

The park now includes an area west of the lakes with numerous unmarked trails. Access is possible via Bellamy Road; via Millstream and Treanor Roads at Bellamy; via Millstream Road at Lost Lake Road; and via Highland Road at Barker Road (where parking space is very limited indeed). Going NW from the Upper Lake an excellent hike can be made to Scafe Hill, with good views from both its summits. From here, with pre-arranged transportation, one can hike out to Millstream Road.

The City of Victoria administers the park, with trail maintenance help from members of the Thetis Lake Nature Sanctuary Association. In spring this group conducts tours of the sanctuary. Their booklet **"Natural History of Thetis Lake"** is available; phone 479-7920. A few years ago Ron Seaborn researched and compiled the trails information and donated this to us and to the City of Victoria Parks Branch for its descriptive leaflet.

Note:

* Trails lead to Freeman King Park; to Mill Hill Park; and to the abandoned C.N.R. right-of-way.

* Be careful with fire. The moss gets very dry in summer and is easily ignited.

* Please take out your garbage.

* **Don't pick the flowers.**

48

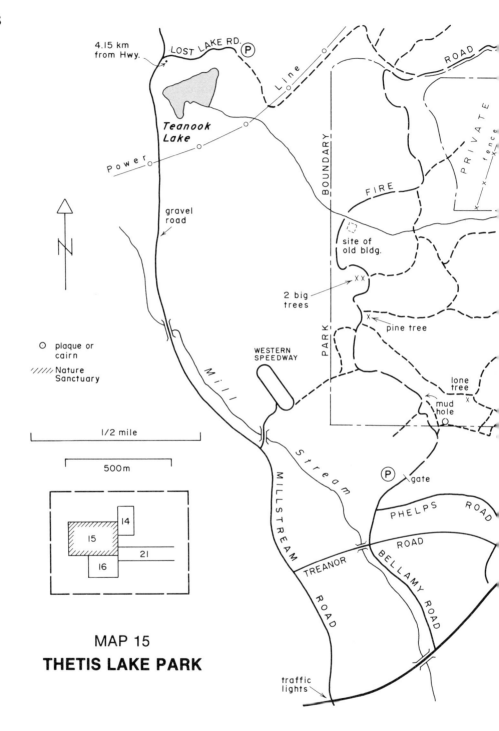

MAP 15
THETIS LAKE PARK

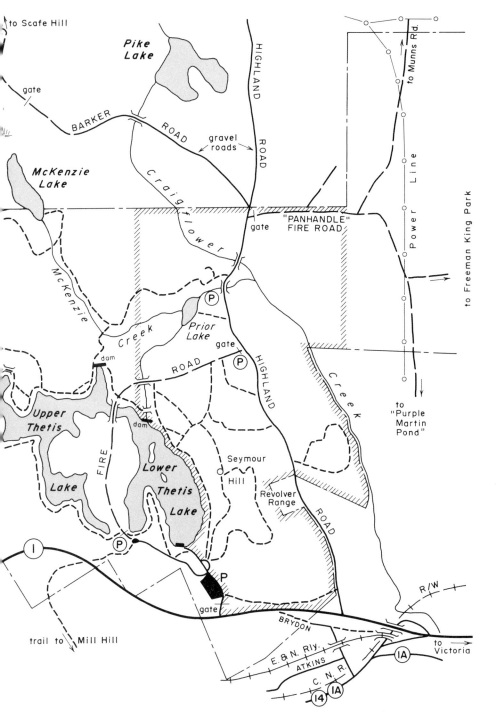

50

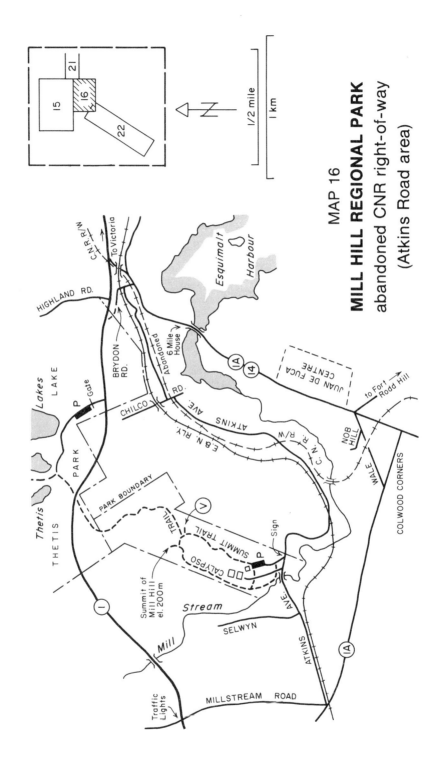

MAP 16
MILL HILL REGIONAL PARK
abandoned CNR right-of-way
(Atkins Road area)

MILL HILL REGIONAL PARK AND C.N.R. RIGHT-OF-WAY

From Victoria on Highway #1 drive 12 km to traffic lights at Millstream Road and turn left. Turn left again onto Atkins Road. Continue over Mill Stream Bridge; then, after the turnoff to CRD Parks Headquarters, turn up left to the large parking lot.

Mill Hill Park (49 hectares) is a good place for early spring flowers and in the shaded areas you will find the Calypso Orchid. Time up to the viewpoint on the Calypso Trail is about 20 minutes. Alternatively, a rocky road leads up to the summit, the site of an old lookout tower from where there are excellent 360° views. You may sometimes find the Calypso Trail indistinct at the summit. If continuing north, stay on the ridge as long as possible before the trail heads down to Highway #1 (no parking here). Time down - 15 minutes. Find trail to Thetis Lake Park across highway. A CRD brochure is available.

Note the C.N.R. right-of-way from the Highway Interchange. For description see page 67.

GOLDSTREAM PROVINCIAL PARK

Just over 16 km from Victoria, Highway #1 winds its way through Goldstream Park (327 hectares) which rises majestically on either hand. There are many parking areas. A B.C. Provincial Parks brochure is available.

The park's diverse terrain (from rain forest to dry ridges of arbutus and pine) attracts groups of all ages. There are many interconnecting forest trails with viewpoints and points of interest which are marked on our map. The Niagara Falls, viewed from the trail below, are a most spectacular sight, particularly in the spring when they are in full spate. In summer the Nature House in the Flats is always busy. Talks are also arranged for visitors at the meeting place in the campground. In the late fall crowds gather along the whole stretch of Goldstream River to watch the returning salmon spawn. Year round you can hike on the trails.

If you are more ambitious climb Mount Finlayson, which offers an excellent view and is well known locally by those in need of vigorous exercise. Time up - 40 to 60 minutes. Stay on the marked trails and avoid the steep, west face which has slippery, crumbly ledges. On a very hot day it may be cooler to make your return on the NW side -- well marked but less frequented. If hiking alone, you are wiser to return on the south trail. Carry your own water. (Note that Mount Finlayson is outside the park.)

Skirt Mountain, south of Mount Finlayson, has several mining claims and mine workings. It is not advisable to hike here with small dogs or small children.

The B.C. Provincial Parks Branch constructed some of the trails. The Outdoor Club of Victoria with Parks Branch assistance built the Arbutus Ridge, Gold Mine, Prospectors and Riverside Trails, and maintains them with periodic volunteer work parties. The South Vancouver Island Rangers, a search and rescue group, built and maintain the Mount Finlayson Trails.

Attention all dogs and cats!
You must keep your human
on a leash in this park.

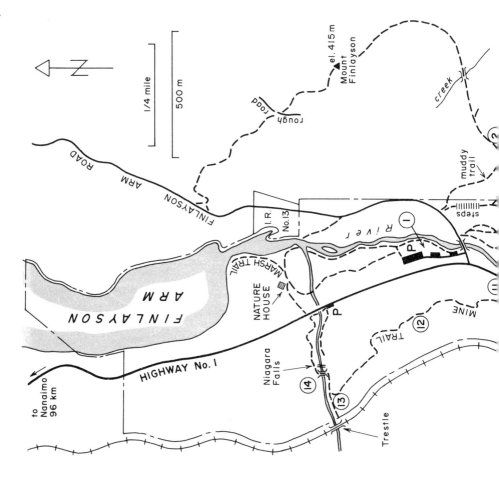

to Nanaimo 96 km

HIGHWAY No. 1

FINLAYSON ARM ROAD

FINLAYSON ARM

rough road

el. 415 m
Mount Finlayson

creek

muddy trail

steps

I.R. No.13

River

MARSH TRAIL

NATURE HOUSE

P

MINE TRAIL

Niagara Falls

Trestle

1/4 mile

500 m

N

MAP 17
GOLDSTREAM
PROVINCIAL PARK
MOUNT FINLAYSON

(14) Bridge at Niagara Canyon above Niagara Falls. Spectacular view of Falls (47-metre drop) in spring if approached from lower trail. No connection between trails at the falls. **Caution: steep slopes in this area.**

(13) View of Finlayson Arm.

(12) Old mine workings. 16-metre tunnel (adit): 7-metre shaft. Quartz outcroppings along trail.

(11) Miners' spring.

(10) Lookout Rock - good views of Mount Finlayson and Skirt Mountain.

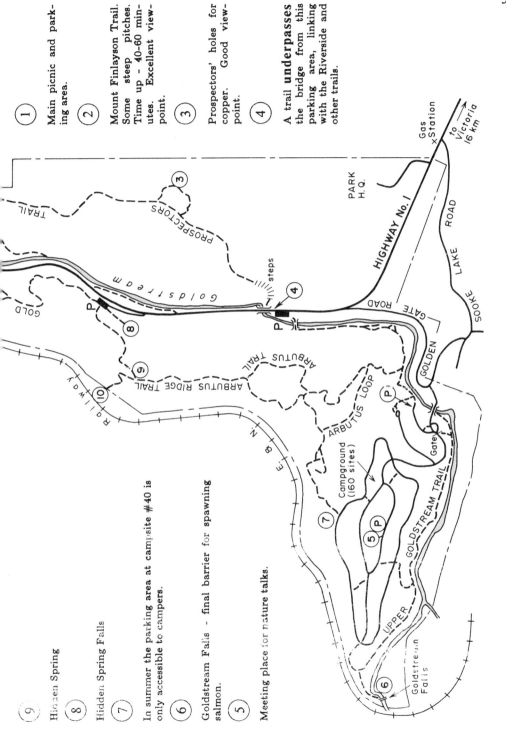

1. Main picnic and parking area.

2. Mount Finlayson Trail. Some steep pitches. Time up - 40-60 minutes. Excellent viewpoint.

3. Prospectors' holes for copper. Good viewpoint.

4. A trail **underpasses** the bridge from this parking area, linking with the Riverside and other trails.

9. Hidden Spring

8. Hidden Spring Falls

7. In summer the parking area at campsite #40 is only accessible to campers.

6. Goldstream Falls - final barrier for spawning salmon.

5. Meeting place for nature talks.

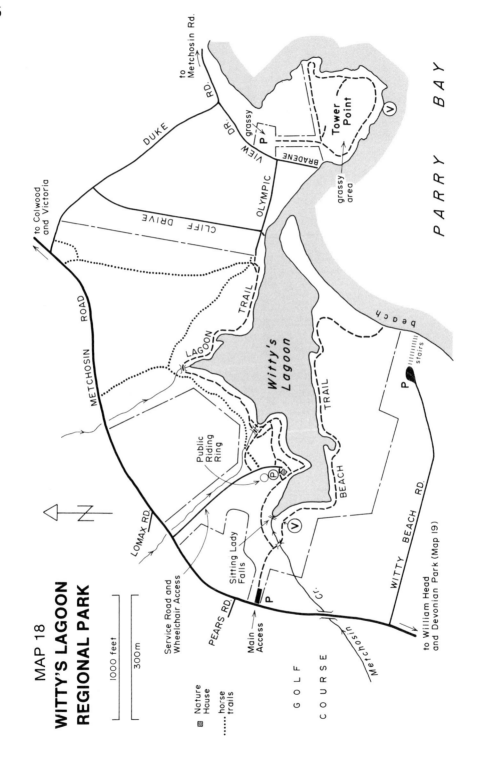

MAP 18
WITTY'S LAGOON
REGIONAL PARK

1000 feet

300m

▨ Nature
House

······· horse
trails

Service Road and
Wheelchair Access

Public
Riding
Ring

Sitting Lady
Falls

Main
Access

P

PEARS RD.

LOMAX RD.

METCHOSIN   ROAD

to Colwood
and Victoria

DUKE   RD.

CLIFF   DRIVE

VIEW   DR.

OLYMPIC

BRAEDNE

to
Metchosin Rd.

grassy

P

Tower
Point

V

grassy
area

LAGOON   TRAIL

Witty's
Lagoon

TRAIL

BEACH

beach

stairs

P

V

GOLF

COURSE

Metchosin

WITTY   BEACH   RD.

to William Head
and Devonian Park (Map 19)

PARRY   BAY

PARRY   BAY

WITTY'S LAGOON REGIONAL PARK

Access from Victoria is via Highways #1 and #14, then turn onto Metchosin Road. Follow this for about 6 km to Pears Road--the main entrance to the park and Nature House--where there is ample parking. Allow about 45 minutes' driving time from Victoria. Other more limited parking areas are shown on our map. Note that there is access for wheelchairs via the service road during hours when the Nature House is in operation, and by request; phone 478-3344. There is a special toilet facility for the disabled by the Nature House. Regular parks facilities will be found here and at Tower Point.

No fires or overnight camping are permitted.

Horses should stay on the designated horse trails or roads.

The park (51 hectares) is an interesting combination of forest, grassland, salt marsh, beach, lagoon and rocky shore, with many birds and plants in these various habitats. Sitting Lady Falls can be spectacular in winter and spring after heavy rain. A CRD brochure is available.

A hike along the beach from here to Taylor Road or Devonian Park is possible.

MAP 19 - DEVONIAN REGIONAL PARK

Access from Victoria is by Highways #1 and #14, then by Metchosin Road and William Head Road -- about 50 minutes' drive from Victoria. See also Map 23. About 500 metres beyond Taylor Road you will find Devonian Park (13 hectares) with ample parking and other parks facilities. The parking lot area shows evidence of being part of an old farm property, farmed for many years by the Helgeson family. From here to the beach by either hiking trail is about a 30-minute walk, passing through forest and wetlands. Sherwood Pond is a good observation area for birdwatchers.

A 3-km one-way walk is possible from Taylor Beach (a shelving, pebble beach) to Witty's Lagoon. Note that there is also beach access at Taylor Road. A CRD brochure is available.

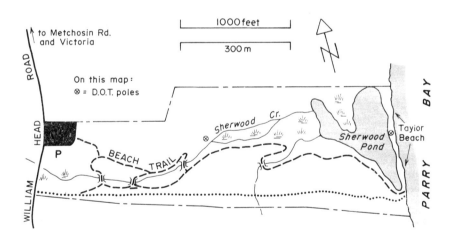

Access from Victoria is via Highways #1 and #14 and thence either by Gillespie Road and East Sooke Road; or via Metchosin, Rocky Point Road and East Sooke Road. The distance to Aylard Farm is about 34 km, an hour's drive from Victoria.

There are five access points to the 1442-hectare park, but note there are only three parking lots with facilities - at Aylard Farm, Anderson Cove and Pike Road. There is limited parking at access D1 and at Coppermine Road, where a 400-metre road brings you to the park gate (unsigned).

This semi-wilderness park is good for year-round hiking offering extensive trails for day hikers within easy reach of Victoria. There are many interconnecting trails, all well-cut and signposted. Distances can be deceptive because of the rough terrain so we give here some approximate hiking times. It is wise to start your hike early in the day and not overestimate your capabilities.

In spring and summer, flower enthusiasts may find the following: fringe cup, orange honeysuckle, stonecrop, monkey flower, hardhack, harvest Brodiaea, white campion, western buttercup, red columbine, small-flower alumroot, white clover, Queen Anne's Lace, Indian paintbrush, seaside woolly sunflower, hedge nettle, clustered wild rose, red elder, mullein, sea blush, Columbia tiger lily, nodding onion and white triteleia.

There is fishing off Beechey Head and at Pike Point. Families of otter living on the rocky beach at Aylard Farm or at Alldridge Point may be seen feeding in the early morning or late evening. You may also see them up and down the Coast Trail. From here seals will be seen frequently and in the summer there can be magnificent viewings of whales. You may see deer at the Aylard Farm end and grouse on the Interior Trail from Babbington Hill onwards.

When hiking in the swampy areas observe the skunk cabbage. In the spring, bears enjoy the centres of skunk cabbages and dandelions. The cougar scratches his territory out like a domestic cat and near the turnoff to Cabin Point there are some alder trees with cougar marks. On the Middle Trail there is quite a raccoon settlement. From the top of Mount Maguire you may see hawks, eagles and pigeons.

For the more energetic hikers the Coast Trail is the best of all. Its scenery is magnificent with good views of the Olympic Peninsula, and the coast itself with deep bays, cliffs and chasms, has an atmosphere of remoteness and adventure.

Families will find hiking from the Aylard Farm end the most rewarding, as there are regular parks facilities, green meadows and good access to sandy beaches; also lookouts at Creyke Point and Beechey Head. Babbington Hill, an excellent viewpoint, is also easily reached from Aylard Farm.

Iron Mine Bay at the west end of the park has a good pebble beach and some fine views.

There is still evidence of old logging roads throughout the peninsula, but in the main our map shows only the officially signposted trails. If you are new to the park you will be well advised to stay on the marked trails. You will find sign boards showing "points of interest". Please do not damage or remove any of these signs.

Note:

* Do not hike alone. Allow time to get out before nightfall.

* There are few creeks, so always carry water.

* Carry a map. A CRD brochure is available.

* **No camping and no fires are permitted.**

* Carry your own litter out.

* At Anderson Cove (from Discovery Road westward almost to Executive Drive) the waterfront area is also included in the park--a useful picnic site.

* For approximate hiking times in the park turn to page 64.

On this map :

- – – moderate trails
.... rugged trails
⛺ shelter
⚒ mine

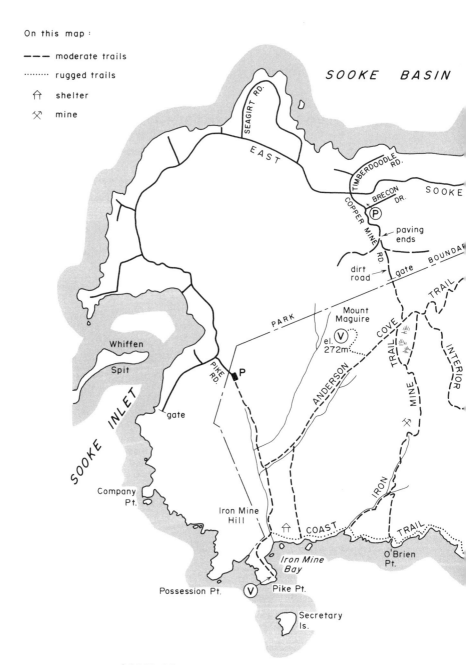

MAP 20
EAST SOOKE REGIONAL PARK

STRAIT OF JUAN DE FUCA

Approximate hiking times in East Sooke Park: **Hours**

Aylard Farm to Pike Road parking lot	6½
Aylard Farm to Beechey Head, via coast	1
Beechey Head to Cabin Point	1½
Cabin Point to Iron Mine Bay	3
Iron Mine Bay to Pike Road parking lot	½
Pike Road parking lot to Anderson Cove, via Anderson Cove Trail	2
Pike Road parking lot to shelter at Iron Mine Bay	½
Pike Road parking lot to Mount Maguire	1
Iron Mine Trail to Interior Trail, from coast	1
Middle Trail to Interior Trail, from coast	½
Anderson Cove Trail to Middle Trail, via Babbington Hill Trail	1¼
Anderson Cove to Babbington Hill	2
Interior Trail, from Anderson Cove Trail to Middle Trail	1¼
Aylard Farm to Babbington Hill	1¼
D1 (at East Sooke Road) to Babbington Hill	1¼

ABANDONED CANADIAN NATIONAL RAILWAY
RIGHT-OF-WAY

This is currently (1986) administered by the B.C. Ministry of Transportation and Highways. Agreement in principle has been reached that the Capital Regional District (CRD) should develop it as a linear park--part of the cross-regional trail system--from Atkins Road west to Shawnigan. Our maps include the area from the Tillicum Mall to the Highway Interchange (not part of the current proposal), plus Atkins Road westward to Leechtown. The CRD proposals for development include provision of toilet facilities and litter bins and the construction of foot-bridges where trestles have been removed. A city map and a map of the Metchosin area would be useful adjuncts to the information given here.

In 1943 the Vancouver Island Division of the C.N.R. consisted of 160 km of track but railways gradually fell into disuse. In 1978 preservation of the right-of-way was requested as a transportation corridor and on most of it (certainly from Tillicum to Sooke) the tracks and ties were removed in 1983.

The right-of-way now offers pleasant urban walks and although never far from a highway, it removes one from the hurly-burly, with surprising glimpses of animal life, hedgerow flowers when in season and sometimes beautiful lookout points. In the interests of safety all trestles have been removed, currently making some sections difficult, but usually if creeks are not too high a crossing can be made, or one can go around on local roads. Apart from these crossings the right-of-way is excellently graded and being well gravelled, is firm of footing. Many trails lead off from the right-of-way onto private land. Stay on it within the fenced area. Most householders along the way own large, fierce-sounding watchdogs! At present (1986) there are no washroom facilities along the way except at shopping centres or where the right-of-way passes through parks. There are no garbage cans, so please do not litter the right-of-way.

Hikers, horsemen and cyclists may use the right-of-way, but no motorized vehicles are permitted.

Note that our maps are not all at the same scale.

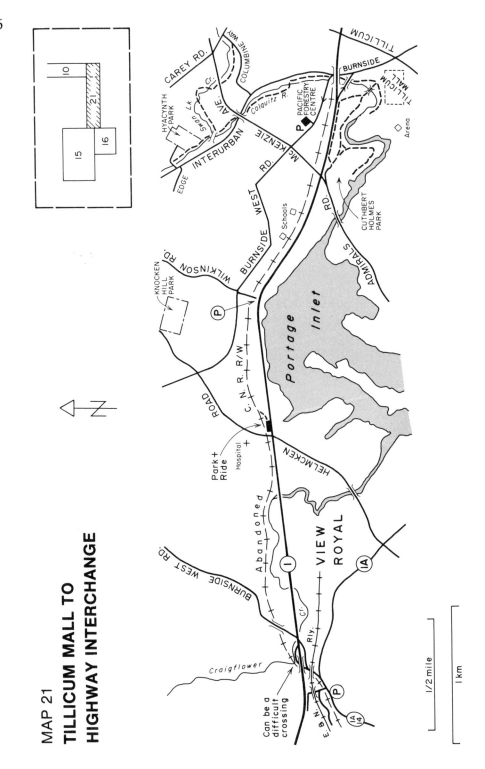

MAP 21
**TILLICUM MALL TO
HIGHWAY INTERCHANGE**

Map 21 - Tillicum Mall to Highway Interchange (4 km) - Not part of the current proposal

From the Tillicum Mall take the trail paralleling Highway #1 to Admirals/McKenzie and cross Highway #1 to pick up the abandoned right-of-way. Or park at the federal Pacific Forestry Centre on Burnside Road (visitor's parking) and pick up the right-of-way from there. The section westward from McKenzie Avenue goes high above the highway with a fine view over Portage Inlet. At Helmcken Road via the Park-and-Ride parking lot pick up the right-of-way again which now veers away from the highway, overhung with trees and seems remote from habitation.

Craigflower Creek must be crossed. Unless a bridge is improvised this would have to be forded when the creek is high. At the Highway Interchange immediately under the bridge you have a choice. The right-of-way continues on to Colwood Corners, but there is also a trail off to the right leading to Brydon Road and thence to Thetis Lake Park or Mill Hill Park.

Map 16 - Highway Interchange to Colwood Corners (3 km)

See page 50. If you choose to continue to Colwood Corners Shopping Centre (at intersection of Highways #14 and #1A), note that currently (1986) there is a flooded, overgrown piece of right-of-way behind Six-Mile House. You can get around this by Atkins Avenue at Chilco Road and it is a rather pleasant section (about a half-hour walk to Colwood Corners).

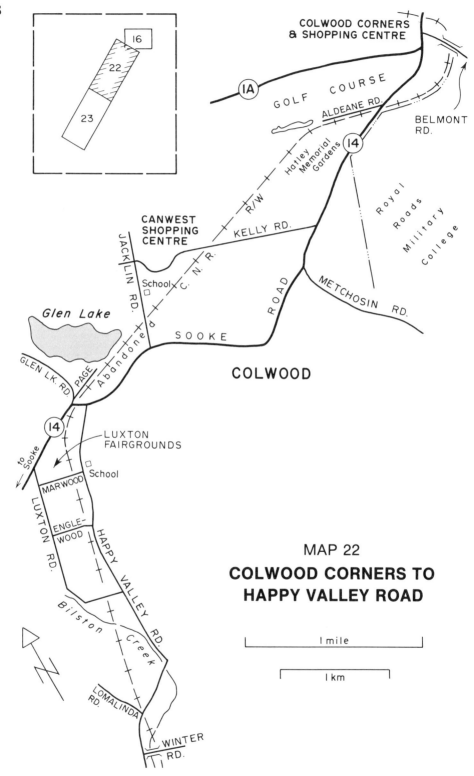

16

22

23

COLWOOD CORNERS
& SHOPPING CENTRE

1A
GOLF COURSE

ALDEANE RD.

14

BELMONT
RD.

Hatley
Memorial
Gardens

R/W

Royal
Roads
Military
College

CANWEST
SHOPPING
CENTRE

KELLY RD.

JACKLIN RD.

C. N. R.

School

METCHOSIN RD.

ROAD

Glen Lake

SOOKE

COLWOOD

GLEN LK. RD.

PAGE

Abandoned

14

to Sooke

LUXTON
FAIRGROUNDS

School

MARWOOD

LUXTON RD.

ENGLE-
WOOD

HAPPY VALLEY RD.

MAP 22

**COLWOOD CORNERS TO
HAPPY VALLEY ROAD**

Bilston Creek

1 mile

1 km

LOMALINDA
RD.

WINTER
RD.

Map 22 - Colwood Corners to Happy Valley Road (9 km)

At Colwood Corners the right-of-way crosses Highway #1A. Under the Belmont Bridge there is currently (1986) another flooded, overgrown section of the right-of-way. At Royal Roads College the right-of-way crosses Highway #14, following along Aldeane Road, behind Hatley Memorial Gardens and continuing straight ahead southwest, recrossing the highway at Glen Lake Road. It passes Luxton Fairgrounds and then more or less follows Happy Valley Road. As currently (1986) there is no bridge at Bilston Creek, detour at Luxton Road onto Happy Valley Road and pick up right-of-way at Lomalinda. Other detours may also be necessary before reaching Glen Forest Way.

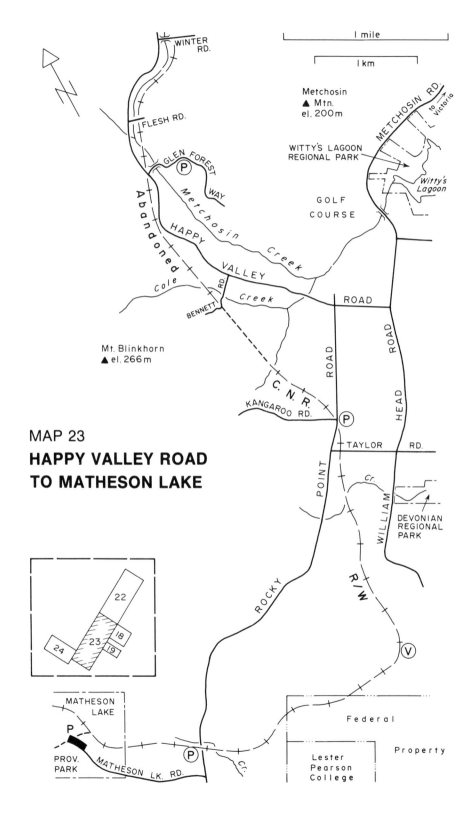

WINTER RD.

FLESH RD.

1 mile

1 km

Metchosin
▲ Mtn.
el. 200m

GLEN FOREST

P

WAY

Abandoned

Metchosin

HAPPY

Creek

VALLEY

WITTY'S LAGOON
REGIONAL PARK

METCHOSIN RD.

to Victoria

Witty's
Lagoon

GOLF
COURSE

Cole

Creek

Creek

BENNETT

RD.

ROAD

Mt. Blinkhorn
▲ el. 266m

C. N. R.

KANGAROO RD.

ROAD

P

TAYLOR

RD.

ROAD

HEAD

Cr.

WILLIAM

DEVONIAN
REGIONAL
PARK

MAP 23

**HAPPY VALLEY ROAD
TO MATHESON LAKE**

POINT

R/W

ROCKY

V

22

24

23

18

19

Federal

Property

MATHESON
LAKE

P

PROV.
PARK

MATHESON LK. RD.

P

Cr.

Lester
Pearson
College

Map 23 - Happy Valley Road to Matheson Lake Park (7 km)

On Happy Valley Road look for Glen Forest Way (after Winter and Flesh Roads), where there is parking for a few cars. This is a very pleasant section of the right-of-way with a fine view of Mount Blinkhorn and further on where the right-of-way swings westward, a beautiful view over Parry Bay. You may see deer and rabbits and in high summer will find wild strawberries. End your walk at Rocky Point Road (limited parking), or continue on to Matheson Lake Park (another 1.5 km), where a trail leads to the parking lot.

72

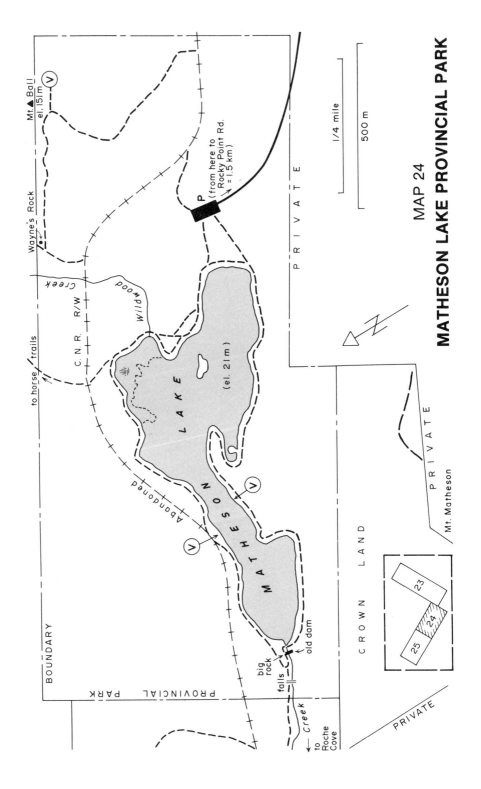

MAP 24
MATHESON LAKE PROVINCIAL PARK

MATHESON LAKE PROVINCIAL PARK

Access from Victoria is via Highway #14 - Metchosin Road - Happy Valley Road - and Rocky Point Road (29 km). Just before the road forks, turn right onto Matheson Lake Park Road (signposted) and about 1.5 km brings you to the parking lot -- about an hour's drive from Victoria.

No fires or camping are permitted in the park (160 hectares) but there are toilet facilities, plus swimming and some fishing. The SE corner of the lake is the best place to launch canoes, but motor boats are not allowed.

The CNR right-of-way links the park to Roche Cove (4.5 km one way). Trails circle Matheson Lake and from the right-of-way at Wildwood Creek a trail leads up to Wayne's Rock (about 15 minutes' walk). Wildwood Creek has three forks and in the area just north of our map several horse trails have been developed. Just beyond Wayne's Rock a trail leads W over the creek and in 15 minutes brings you again to the right-of-way.

Trails lead up to Mount Ball from whose summit the view is northward to Mount Redflag. A good viewpoint is also shown on our map towards Victoria and the sea.

The trail along the creek from Matheson Lake to Roche Cove was the old timers' portage trail in the 1850s and '60s.

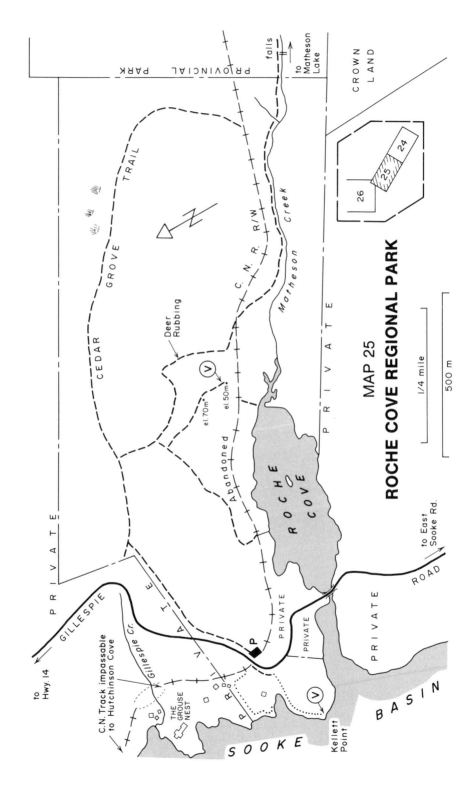

MAP 25
ROCHE COVE REGIONAL PARK

1/4 mile

500 m

ROCHE COVE REGIONAL PARK

Access to Roche Cove Park (117 hectares) is by Highway #14. Just past 17 Mile House turn left onto Gillespie Road and 3 km will bring you to the parking lot which has toilet facilities. It is about a 45-minute drive from Victoria.

Cross the road and go on foot past the barrier to the walk-in picnic area. The road ahead leads to the coast past the caretaker's residence on your left. Yellow markers show clearly the boundary of the park and the Grouse Nest private property beyond. A walk northward is possible on the CNR right-of-way, which comes to an abrupt end where the trestle has been removed. Currently, (1986) the right-of-way is impassable from here to Veitch Creek.

Returning to the barrier, a trail immediately to your left leads to Kellett Point, three beaches, lovely grassy slopes and beautiful views of the Sooke Basin and Olympic Mountains. It is an excellent picnic area.

Recross the road into the greater part of Roche Cove Park where you can continue on the right-of-way or follow the Matheson Creek Trail into Matheson Lake Park; or explore other trails recently created from older roads. An especially good viewpoint is shown on our map NE of Roche Cove. Note an area where a large buck has rubbed the velvet off his horns. He must be quite old as there are signs of his rubbing from previous years.

CNR RIGHT-OF-WAY, VEITCH CREEK TO LEECHTOWN (22 KM); EMPRESS MOUNTAIN, SOOKE HILLS AREA

An interesting section of the right-of-way starts at Veitch Creek (Hutchinson Cove), via Manzer Road just past Glinz Lake Road. Distance from Victoria is about 30 km. The right-of-way along here seems almost to hang out over the water and it must have been a memorable train ride in bygone days. From Veitch Creek to Sooke Potholes Provincial Park is 10 km one way, about a 2-hour hike. Crossing Ayum Creek may sometimes be difficult; if so, detour by Ludlow Road and Highway #14 to Harbour View Road.

The Sooke River Railway Preservation Society, a group of railway buffs, operates a train service on 5 km of track between Milnes Landing Station and Barnes Station. Trains generally run on weekends and may also operate on certain weekdays. Rides on "railway speeders" or "track motors" can be arranged during the summer or at any time by special arrangement; phone 478-5655 or 598-5511. The tracks and ties continue for another 800 m beyond Barnes Station and from here a 7-km hike brings you to the old goldmining ghost town of Leechtown. By arrangement the train could pick you up on your return. Hikers may hike along the Railway Society's tracks but should use caution at all times. Those who feel unhappy about heights should note that there is a high trestle over the Charters River. At the Todd Creek trestle trails lead down to the Potholes Park.

Sooke Potholes Provincial Park is a delightful spot for swimming and picnicking and the area round about on both sides of the river is well worth exploring.

The YM-YWCA have developed some good bush trails around Camp Thunderbird, all signposted. You may hike there from mid-October to mid-April, but should obtain their permission before doing so; phone 386-7511.

Harrison Trail (a rough old road) leads up towards the top of Empress Mountain from the Sooke Potholes and the view from the top (673 m) can be spectacular. During the past two years a great deal of logging has taken place in this area--also around Ragged Mountain, Crabapple Lake and Mount Manuel Quimper. Harbour View Road is now a fairly well maintained logging road, open to the public except during periods of fire hazard.

The top of Empress Mountain is Crown land. Much of the area is owned by Canadian Industrial Products, Inc. and Western Forest Products Ltd. also have some holdings. Both these companies make their recreational leaflets available. See also National Topographic Map 92B/5 (available from Maps B.C.) and Outdoor Recreation Council Map #15. For information on all the above see page 91. Vancouver-based Acadia Heights Development Ltd. have holdings in the Mount Manuel Quimper/Crabapple Lake area.

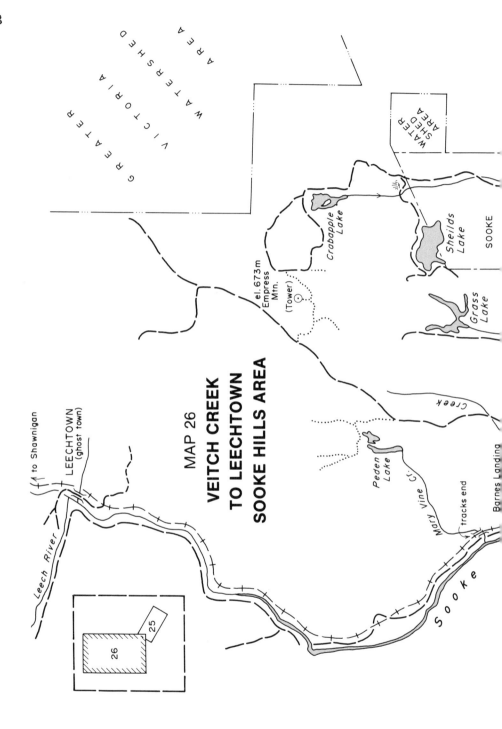

GREATER VICTORIA WATERSHED AREA

WATER SHED AREA

SOOKE

Crabapple Lake

Sheilds Lake

Grass Lake

el. 673m
Empress Mtn.
⊙ (Tower)

Creek

MAP 26

**VEITCH CREEK
TO LEECHTOWN
SOOKE HILLS AREA**

Peden Lake

Mary Vine Cr

tracks end

Barnes Landing

Sooke

to Shawnigan

LEECHTOWN
(ghost town)

Leech River

25

26

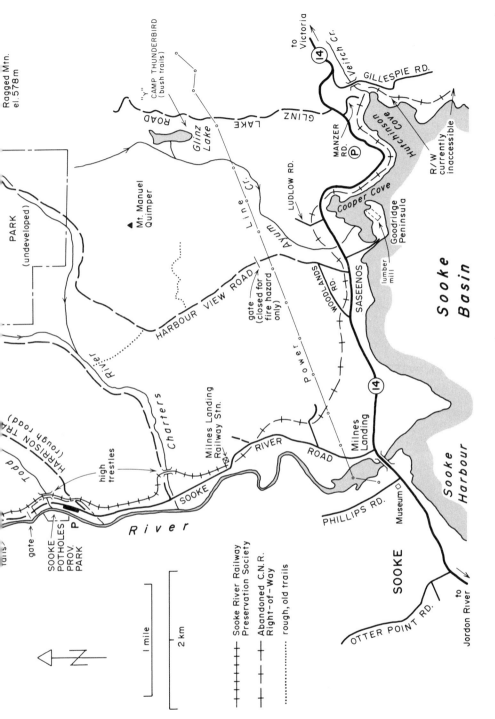

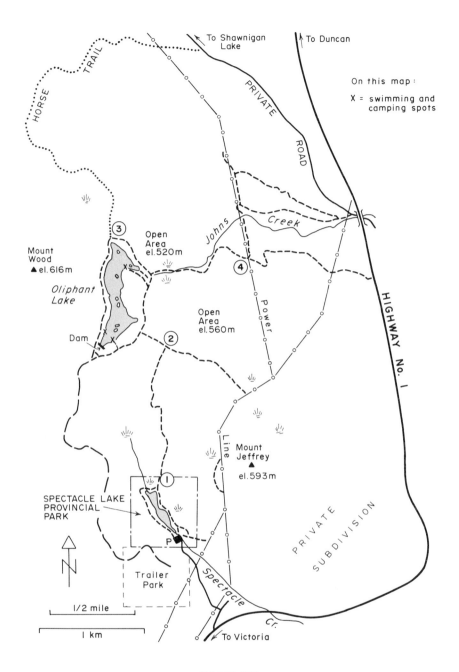

MAP 27
SPECTACLE LAKE PROVINCIAL PARK
OLIPHANT LAKE

SPECTACLE LAKE PROVINCIAL PARK
AND OLIPHANT LAKE

On Highway #1 travelling N past the first Shawnigan Lake cutoff, continue .8 km then turn left onto Whitaker Road--signposted to Spectacle Lake Park (65 hectares). About 1 km more brings you to the parking lot. There are parks facilities but no camping is permitted.

Spectacle Lake (so named as it resembles a pair of spectacles) is a pretty little lake, good for swimming and a walk around it takes about half an hour. It is said to have eastern brook trout in it.

A good hike is possible from here to Oliphant Lake which is harder to find, as for the most part it is not visible from its eastern side. Follow the trail on the east side of Spectacle Lake and continue N on a pleasant woodsy trail ① ascending gradually for about 30 minutes to a T junction ②.

About 10 minutes hike to your left will bring you to a rough road. A right or left turn will lead you to the trails around Oliphant Lake. There is access to three good swimming and camping spots as shown on our map. At the north arm of the lake ③ a horse trail continues N, then W, and then veers NE crossing the power line nearly 2 km north of Johns Creek. Just south of the creek at ④ there is an excellent view of the Saanich Inlet. Other pleasant views can be found by picking your own route up to the open areas shown. Mount Wood is the highest point of the Malahat Ridge.

If returning via the powerline, you might miss the trail leading back to the T junction ②, but the power line will lead you back to the Spectacle Lake parking lot. Crossing the creek is sometimes difficult, but there is a little trail to the right leading to the main trail.

The route via ① ② ③ ② ① with a side trip to the viewpoint at the north end of the lake takes about four hours.

A rough road (4-wheel drive vehicles only) leads south from Oliphant Lake back to Spectacle Lake via the trailer park.

Spectacle/Oliphant Lakes cont'd.

The rare mountain quail may be seen along the power line.

See also National Topographic Map 92B/12 and Outdoor Recreation Council Map #15. For information on these see page 91.

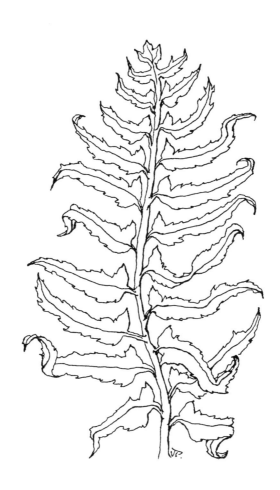

BEACH ACCESS FROM HIGHWAY #14
WEST OF SOOKE
(for locations see Table of Contents, p.6)

French Beach Provincial Park

About an hour's drive from Victoria (21.5 km west of Sooke Centre); or 8.2 km west of Muir Creek Bridge. Ample parking. Parks facilities include 69 campsites. Easy trails and a beautiful sandy beach.

Juan de Fuca Viewpoint (in Western Forest Products Ltd. Tree Farm Licence 25)

Just over 2 km west of French Beach Park turn onto gravel road leading to a small parking lot. From here a 5-minute, level trail leads to a picnic area and viewpoint. Not exactly a beach--rocky and with grassy spots.

Sandcut Creek Trail (in WFP Ltd. TFL 25)

From Victoria, 65 km, (nearly a 90-minute drive), or from Point No Point Resort 3.7 km to the parking lot. No facilities. A pretty rain forest trail with easy descent leads to a long expanse of sand and pebble beach. Time down - about 10 minutes; up - about 15 minutes. A beach walk from here to Jordan River is about 3 km one way.

Jordan River picnic site (WFP Ltd.)

At the mouth of the Jordan River, about 90 minutes' drive from Victoria, (74 km), Western Forest Products Ltd. has provided a parking and picnic area large enough to accommodate campers and trailers, with parks facilities.

China Beach Provincial Park

Just over 90 minutes' drive from Victoria. From Jordan River Bridge it is 4 km to the ample China Beach parking lot. A good trail, fairly steep, but well graded and suitable for family hikers, leads down through rain forest to a long sandy beach. There are toilet facilities but no camping is permitted. Time down - 15 minutes; up - about 25 minutes.

Mystic Beach Trail (WFP Ltd., TFL 25)

5.8 km west of Jordan River Bridge, find parking area. No other facilities. This steep trail (about 1.5 km through rain forest) was upgraded in 1986 by the Company. Time down - about 15 minutes; up - about 25 minutes.

Map 28 - Sombrio Beach Trails (WFP Ltd., TFL 25)

From Victoria it is roughly 90 km, a two-hour drive, to the Sombrio area. Two trails lead down to the beach and the Company advises these will both be signposted from the highway in 1987.

(1) 23 km west of Jordan River on Highway #14 turn left onto a logging spur road and drive straight ahead for about 1 km to a parking area. The trail from here is steep and currently rough. It can be very muddy. Time down to beach - about 15 minutes; up - about 20-25 minutes.

(2) On Highway #14 after a further km westward, turn left onto a logging spur road. After 1 km turn sharply left again and continue to parking area. From here there is an easy five-minute walk to a beautiful, sandy and rocky beach, typical of Vancouver Island's west coast.

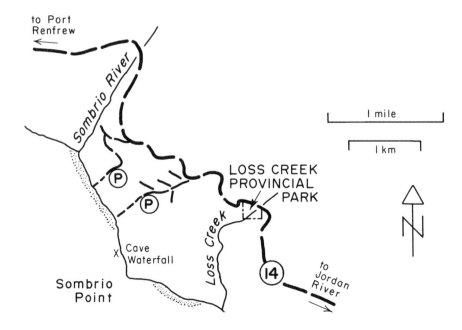

A brochure **"Visitors' Guide to Jordan River Area"** with information on all these areas is available from Western Forest Products Ltd. (for address see page 91). Obey all posted signs. Access may be closed when fire hazard is high. The Company intends to do some maintenance work on all their trails in 1987 as funds permit.

MAP 29
BOTANICAL BEACH, PORT RENFREW

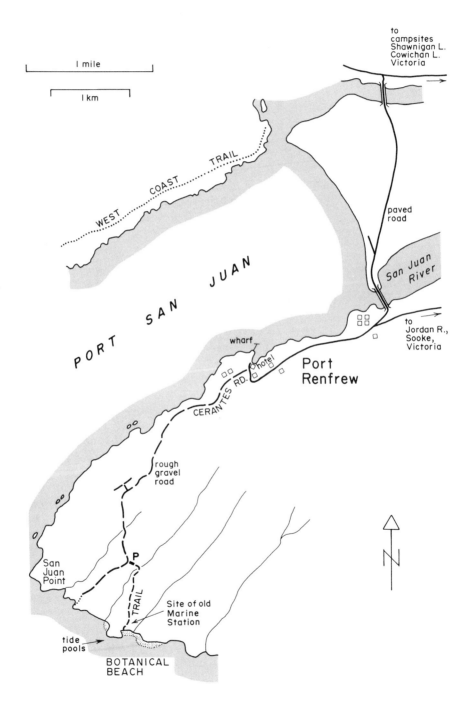

I mile

I km

to
campsites
Shawnigan L.
Cowichan L.
Victoria

WEST COAST TRAIL

paved
road

San Juan
River

PORT SAN JUAN

to
Jordan R.,
Sooke,
Victoria

wharf

hotel

CERANTES RD.

Port
Renfrew

rough
gravel
road

San
Juan
Point

P

TRAIL

Site of old
Marine
Station

N

tide
pools

BOTANICAL
BEACH

Botanical Beach is located on the west coast of southern Vancouver Island near Port Renfrew, about 113 km from Victoria.

This unique beach area, with tidal pools filled with a variety of marine life, is of particular interest to marine biologists and other naturalists. Various universities conduct biological studies here; they request that marine life not be disturbed. Since a low tide is most desirable for visiting this area, check tide tables. Obtain **"Pacific Coast Tide and Current Tables" Volume 6** and refer to tides at Tofino, using correction for Port Renfrew. (This is available from Institute of Ocean Sciences, Canadian Hydrographic Service, P.O. Box 6000, Sidney, B.C. V8L 4B2, or at bookstores and sporting goods stores; also available from public libraries.)

Note that cold water precludes swimming here. This is not a park and there are no facilities. Creeks provide drinking water. Rubber boots are useful when the trail is wet.

Access: Drive to Port Renfrew from Victoria via Sooke and Jordan River, or from Shawnigan Lake or Cowichan Lake. Roads are mostly gravel and usually in fair to good condition. It takes over two hours to drive from Victoria to Port Renfrew via Jordan River--the best route for cars with most of the route paved. Turn left on small, rough road (Cerantes Road) just before reaching Port Renfrew Hotel and government wharf. Follow road by vehicle as far as possible, then walk.

The road from Port Renfrew to the beach is about 5 km long, entirely through private lands. It is probably passable to most vehicles for the first 3 km. Beyond that the road has deteriorated until it is really only a good trail, not recommended even for most 4-wheel drive vehicles. Washouts may block it entirely.

By car, watch your odometer from the turnoff at the hotel and follow the main route until 3.2 km, at which point there will be a road uphill to the left (east). At the crest of the hill there is room for about seven cars to park; the road (trail) continues to the beach--a brisk 10-minute walk. If you follow the main road past the above junction to the right, you will arrive at another beach reached by a short trail from a parking area.

Note:

*   Take care not to be cut off from safe return from beach hikes by rising tides ... cliffs are very steep in some places. Rocks on beach can be very slippery.

*   At Botanical Beach a small area (2 hectares) has been purchased by the Nature Conservancy of Canada. This property is the original site of the University of Minnesota marine station established in 1900.

This can be accessed from Port Renfrew (see Map 29). Write to Pacific Rim National Park, P.O. Box 280, Ucluelet, B.C. V0R 3A0 for a useful leaflet on the West Coast Trail. They can also supply up-to-date information before the start of your trip. For tide table information see page 87. A special waterproof topographic map of the West Coast Trail (Scale 1:50,000) is available from Maps B.C. (for address see page 90). A book, **"The Pacific Rim Explorer - the Complete Guide"** by Bruce Obee, published by Whitecap Books (1986), price $9.95, will help prepare you for your trip with comprehensive material. This book also includes the Nitinat Triangle, the Broken Islands, Barkley Sound, Long Beach and the coastal area up to and including Hot Springs Cove.

The Pack and Boots Shop in Victoria (for address see page 91) has a notice board and can help hikers to find trekking partners.

CLUB ADDRESSES

For information on the Outdoor Club of Victoria, or for the Vancouver Island Section of the Alpine Club of Canada, contact the Victoria Public Library.

For information on Club Tread, contact the Victoria Public Library or the Pack and Boots Shop (see page opposite).

For information on the Island Mountain Ramblers, write to P.O. Box 691, Nanaimo, B. C. V9R 5M2

The Alpine Club and the Ramblers have district representatives.

USEFUL ADDRESSES AND INFORMATION

Maps BC
Ministry of Environment and Parks
Parliament Buildings
Victoria, B.C. V8V 1X5   387-1441

    (or in person at Room 110, 553 Superior Street,
    Victoria, 9 am - 4 pm weekdays)

B.C. Parks and Outdoor Recreation Division   387-5002
Ministry of Environment and Parks

Information Services   387-5255
B.C. Ministry of Forests and Lands

    Both the above at:

    4000 Seymour Place
    Victoria, B.C. V8V 1X4

Capital Regional District
Parks Division
490 Atkins Road
Victoria, B.C. V9B 2Z8   478-3344

Canadian Industrial Products, Inc.
P. O. Box 910
Sooke, B.C. V0S 1N0   642-5237

   (or in person at 7369 Hwy. 14
Sooke, 8 am - 4:30 pm weekdays)

Western Forest Products Ltd.
Jordan River Forest Operation
River Jordan, B.C. V0S 1L0   646-2031

   (or in person at their Forestry Office,
Jordan River, 8 am - 4:30 pm weekdays)

Victoria International Youth Hostel
(Pack and Boots Shop)
516 Yates Street   Hostel: 385-4511
Victoria, B.C. V8W 1K8   Store: 385-5313

Outdoor Recreation Council of B.C.
1200 Hornby Street
Vancouver, B.C. V6Z 2E2   687-1600

   (They have a series of regional maps. In
particular, see Map #15, **"Greater Victoria -
Gulf Islands - Nanaimo Region"**, available at
sporting goods stores - $3.95)

ACKNOWLEDGEMENTS

We are most grateful to the following for the help they have given:

Capital Regional District (Parks Division)
Saanich Municipality
Central Saanich Municipality
North Saanich Municipality
City of Victoria (Parks Branch)
Ministries of B.C. Provincial Government:
        Environment & Parks   (Surveys & Mapping);
                               (Parks & Outdoor Recreation)
        Provincial Secretary   (Archives)
        Transportation and Highways
Canadian Industrial Products, Inc.
Western Forest Products Ltd.

Erma Addison
Stan Buxcey
Johnnie Clay
Hilde Cook
Maurice Danard
Jim Fisher
Bernie Howard
Al Hunter
Eleanor Marcus
Edo Nyland
Barbara Payne
Hugh & Lillian Salmond

Mel Smith
Ron Seaborn
Barney Steel
Sunset Riding Club
Swan Lake Christmas Hill
    Nature Sanctuary
Mollie Thompson
Don Wagg
Alan & Patricia Warren
Ron Weir
Rosa Wood

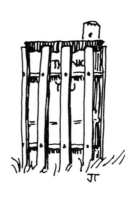

Addresses	90
Beach access west of Sooke	83
Bear Hill Regional Park	32
Beaver Lake	33
Botanical Beach	86
CNR right-of-way	50,65
China Beach Provincial Park	83
Coles Bay Provincial Park	13
Colquitz River Linear Park	34
Devonian Regional Park	59
Durrance Lake	40
East Sooke Regional Park	60
Elk and Beaver Lakes Regional Park	32
Francis/Freeman King Regional Park	43
French Beach Provincial Park	83
Goldstream Provincial Park	52
Hints and Cautions	10
Horth Hill Regional Park	14
Island View Beach Regional Park	28
John Dean Provincial Park	18
Jordan River picnic site	83
Juan de Fuca viewpoint	83
Legend	9
Lochside Drive right-of-way	26
Lone Tree Hill Regional Park	42
McKenzie Bight	40
Matheson Lake Provincial Park	72
Mill Hill Regional Park	50
Mount Douglas Park	24
Mount Work Regional Park	38
Mystic Beach	84
Oliphant Lake	80
Roche Cove Provincial Park	74
Sandcut Creek Trail	83
Sidney Spit Marine Provincial Park	16
Sombrio Beach	84
Swan Lake Nature Sanctuary	37
Spectacle Lake Provincial Park	80
Thetis Lake Park	47
Tide Tables	87
West Coast Trail	89
Willow Way	22
Witty's Lagoon Regional Park	56